Mara Parra

The Modern Mystic's Guide to

TAROT

*A Beginner's Guide to Reading and
Understanding the Cards of the Tarot*

summersdale

Illustrations by
Josefina Schargorodsky

THE MODERN MYSTIC'S GUIDE TO TAROT

Text copyright © Mara Parra, 2024
Illustrations copyright © Josefina Schargorodsky, 2024
First published in 2020 as *Magas Ilustradas* by FERA EDICIONES

Translation by Ivanna Hryc

An Hachette UK Company
www.hachette.co.uk

Summersdale Publishers
Part of Octopus Publishing Group Limited
Carmelite House
50 Victoria Embankment
LONDON
EC4Y 0DZ
UK

www.summersdale.com

Printed and bound in China

ISBN: 978-1-83799-419-9

Substantial discounts on bulk quantities of Summersdale books are available to corporations, professional associations and other organizations. For details contact general enquiries: telephone: +44 (0) 1243 771107 or email: enquiries@summersdale.com.

Foreword

The story of the hero's journey is common in myths and fairy tales. However, it is only through Tarot's major arcana that we find it told using just a series of images. The protagonist of this journey, The Fool, is the perfect example of a person who travels the path of individuation. So, in modern terms, we can define Tarot as a self-knowledge tool.

The Modern Mystic's Guide to Tarot offers a simple way to delve into the study of Tarot and relate it to everyday life. This book is dedicated to women who perform magic without wands – an interesting concept that frees Tarot from its strange and suspicious reputation, and gives it clarity. Tarot is a symbolic language that talks to us about how to develop and achieve personal growth.

I will not elaborate here on the diverse origins of Tarot, as this is covered in the pages that follow, but I would like to expand briefly on the different stages of Tarot.

Those of us who see Tarot as a tale of the hero's journey believe that, through its images, the arcana show the story of a human life and the paths of initiation.

Tarot's major arcana can be interpreted as a representation of the wheel of time or the wheel of life, while the minor arcana present four paths of initiation as shown on The Magician's table. These paths are: the education of willpower (fire), connection to emotions (water), knowledge of universal laws and creative thinking (air), and the ability to control and manipulate (earth).

Tarot teaches us that everything we want to achieve in this world is reached by means of a process related to the number four. Everything begins with an inspiration or idea (The Magician), which requires us to be receptive (The High Priestess). This then moves on to a process of germination or pregnancy (The Empress), which will be shaped in the world (The Emperor).

The journey through the wheel of life is a journey toward wholeness. If we aspire to fully reach our potential, we should make our way through the wheel, from The Fool to The World. We start the journey feeling inconsistent as The Fool and we finish it as a wise fool, or at least that is what the major arcana offer. The arcana are achievements on the path through life, and victories over our own limitations. In order to succeed, we don't need a wand or secret knowledge, but the magic of perseverance and being open to mystery. That is all it takes.

Graciela Caprarulo
Author of *The Oracle of the Hero's Journey*

Contents

INTRODUCTION

Before we look at the Tarot cards in detail, I'd like to invite you on a journey through Tarot history. Although the Tarot deck's origins remain uncertain, it is interesting to see how the use of card reading has related to the popular concepts of each time period since Tarot's inception. We will consider some of the questions people often ask when faced with Tarot. I'll give you my answers to these, but they are just a starting point to help you find your own. Remember, nothing is absolute when it comes to magic. Finally, you will find a helpful guide to numerology. Numbers provide a simple method for remembering the key facts about each arcanum without having to memorize all the meanings. Numerology is also a great way of understanding how the cards are related to each other throughout the deck.

The History of Tarot

The history of Tarot is a mystery that remains unsolved even today. Although the creation of some decks can be traced to as early as four or five centuries ago, the origin of Tarot remains uncertain. It is believed to have begun as a card game, which then acquired symbolism and was later used to predict the future, before it became the self-knowledge tool it is today.

The first playing cards appear to have been brought to Europe by Mediterranean merchants following the Silk Road through China, Persia (now Iran) and part of Africa in the thirteenth century. These decks already consisted of four suits. It is thought that the triumphs (the mythical figures matching the major arcana) were added in Italy. The addition of the triumphs completed a deck of 78 cards that were used in a game called *tarocco*, a trick-taking game, the goal of which was to match the triumph placed facing up. Similar games also existed in Germany and France.

The first records of complete decks date back to the fifteenth century in Italy, where wealthy families from the north commissioned artists to paint personalized cards for them. A well-known example is the Duke of Milan, Filippo María Visconti, who ordered the artist Bonifacio Bembo to create a set of cards as a wedding gift for his daughter Bianca and her spouse, Francesco Sforza. This resulted in the creation of the famous Visconti-Sforza deck, a luxurious golden deck which, despite not being used for divination at that time, laid the foundations for the major and minor arcana of the Marseilles Tarot and all the decks inspired by it.

The Renaissance deck Sola Busca dates back to a similar time and inspired the creation of the widely known English Rider–Waite–Smith Tarot in the early twentieth century. It is believed that the Sola Busca deck may have been commissioned from the artist Nicola di Maestro Antonio by a wealthy Venetian family. Some of the illustrations on these cards refer to historical and mythological events that are less familiar today, which lends the deck a sense of mystery. Incomplete versions of these original Tarot decks from the 1400s exist in private collections and libraries, as well as in some museums such as the Albertina Museum in Vienna and the British Museum in London.

It was not until the eighteenth century that Tarot reading was popularized in France as a means of divination. Its prime promoter was Etteilla, a merchant who had become an occultist. He commissioned a deck that became popular at the time and was harshly criticized by occultists such as Arthur Edward Waite, who considered many of Etteilla's interventions to be whimsical and subjective, twisting the meaning of the cards. He also had supporters, however, such as the French occultist and thinker Antoine Court de Gébelin, who claimed that the major arcana came from the ancient Egyptian book of Thoth. It was he who justified the existence of the 22 cards of the major arcana by associating them with the 22 letters of the Hebrew alphabet. This allowed Etteilla to make a connection between Tarot and astrology, which was accepted by English scholars in the early twentieth century. Interestingly enough, the French occultist orders of the time insisted that Tarot was Egyptian in origin. However, a link has never been found and it is believed that many of the original elements in Tarot do not belong to Egyptian culture and could not have been a product of it, at least not in the way suggested in the first-known cards.

Some believe that, during the eighteenth century, Tarot played a role in the French Revolution. The writer and medium Marie-Anne Lenormand is thought to have read cards for Napoleon, his wife Joséphine and Robespierre, among other influential leaders of the time. Although there is no certainty that it was used by Marie-Anne herself, the "Petit Lenormand" had become popular by 1840 and could well have been her deck of choice. It was not a Tarot deck, but a 36-card oracle containing animals, characters and objects, and it is still in use today.

The Rider–Waite–Smith Tarot was published in 1909 in England. Waite, who was born in Brooklyn, New York, USA, and raised in London, was a member of the Hermetic Order of the Golden Dawn. He commissioned illustrations for the pack from a fellow member, the artist Pamela Colman Smith. The pack was published by Rider, under the publishing house William Rider & Son, which also published an edition of *Dracula*, by Bram Stoker, around that time. The most noticeable change in this deck was introduced by Colman Smith. She chose to illustrate allegorical scenes in all the minor arcana, instead of the simplified drawings showing number and suit found in most decks. Her work was inspired by various decks, such as the Sola Busca, whose three of spades, for example, looks almost identical to the Rider version. On his part, Waite focused on "improving" the design of the major arcana. He changed the order of the Justice and Strength cards to reflect the spirit of astrological signs Libra and Leo, and deleted one of the three characters on The Lovers card to mirror the essence of Gemini. The Rider has become the most popular deck in the Western world, with some 100 million copies sold. However, Colman Smith died in poverty, having received very little money for the illustrations of the 78 arcana and during her life she received no acknowledgement for her talented and inspiring work.

During the same era, when secret orders and esoteric studies were popular in England, the magician Aleister Crowley also created a Tarot deck. As well as being a magician, he was an occultist and, like Edward Waite and Pamela Colman Smith, a member of the Hermetic Order of the Golden Dawn (although, unlike them, he was kicked out due to his scandalous behaviour). Crowley worked on his deck with the artist Frieda Harris, and used references from the ancient book of the Egyptian god Thoth. He maintained the link theorized by Gébelin between the major arcana and Hebrew letters, and the association to astrology developed by Etteilla. Unlike Waite, he did not exchange the order of the Justice and Strength cards, although he did make changes to the names of some arcana. In the Thoth Tarot, Justice is called Adjustment, Strength is Lust, Temperance is Art, Judgement is The Aeon and The World is The Universe.

The Marseilles Tarot enjoyed a surge in popularity in the late twentieth century, largely due to its modernization by the Chilean artist and filmmaker

Alejandro Jodorowsky together with the French Philippe Camoin, who hailed from a family of Tarot card-makers. Jodorowsky claimed to have recreated the most complete and accurate version of the Marseilles Tarot of all time, which he published in a book – written in collaboration with Marianne Costa – called *The Way of Tarot*. Contemporary tarologists use this book as a reference tool for the numerology required to understand the structure of Tarot and much of the symbolism associated with the psychological aspects of it. Jodorowsky was also the creator of psychomagic, a non-scientific spiritual healing method. This technique combines shamanism, psychology, drama, poetry and Tarot to prescribe magical acts, or rituals, designed to address the needs and traumas of the patient. During his research, Jodorowsky came across more than a thousand Tarot decks from different eras. He ended up choosing the Marseilles deck, which includes strong references to ancient Tarot decks, such as the Visconti-Sforza. In his study of the Marseilles deck, Jodorowsky noticed the psychological aspects of the arcana, which led him to state that Tarot is an instrument to observe the present, not the future, and that anyone who claims to be able to predict the future with the cards is conning us.

Ultimately, this confirmed an idea that had been growing since the mid-twentieth century thanks to the development of psychological studies and their application to multiple disciplines. Nowadays, Tarot is seen as a tool to enable self-knowledge and to reflect our present. We can choose to read cards for ourselves or use them to help other people to see themselves when they cannot see their path clearly.

Frequently Asked Questions

What Tarot deck is *Enchantress Tarot* based on?

This book features the cards from the deck that I have created, *Enchantress Tarot*, an empowering deck that helps the reader to embrace their femininity. I always say that *Enchantress Tarot* is a deck that intertwines the best of two Tarot worlds, with pretty sound grounding. The major arcana in this deck correspond to the traditional Marseilles deck. This allows us to work with the archetypes behind each arcanum and follow the numerology theorized by Alejandro Jodorowsky. That's why you'll find our eighth arcanum is Justice and the eleventh is Strength.

In the Rider–Waite–Smith deck, the order of these cards is swapped. As mentioned before, the reason for this is that the cards were related to Hebrew letters associated with an astrological order. This connection will be explained later on, when we describe each card, but here's a brief version: if The Emperor is Aries, The Hierophant is Taurus, The Lovers is Gemini and The Chariot is Cancer, English occultists decided Justice (historically the eighth arcanum) couldn't be Leo, and placed Strength in its place, as it reflected better on the Leo self-energy. Justice then became the eleventh arcanum, matching the characterization of the sign of Libra. Much of this information is found in *The Book of Thoth* which originally came with the Thoth deck by Aleister Crowley. On the renumbering of the Justice and Strength cards, in his book, *The Pictorial Key to the Tarot,* Waite simply states: "As the variation carries nothing with it which will signify to the reader, there is no cause for explanation."

This shows that Tarot decks created in early twentieth-century England were designed with a wider concept of the magic involved, incorporating astrology, mysticism, kabbalah, mythology and alchemy.

Coming back to the design of *Enchantress Tarot,* I must clarify that, although I follow the Marseilles numerology, some illustrations in the major arcana take elements from the Rider–Waite–Smith Tarot, like the tied-up man and woman in The Devil, or the horse in The Sun. We also decided to base our design for the minor arcana on this English deck. To do so, we studied the work done by Pamela Colman Smith in 1909. It is believed that she visited a photography exhibition at the British Museum in London in 1908 – and there she must have seen some black-and-white photos of the Renaissance Italian Tarot Sola Busca. This would explain why her representation of some of the minor arcana is practically identical to that of the fifteenth-century Tarot. Together with Josefina Schargorodsky, the illustrator of our deck, we analyzed Colman Smith's art to turn the minor arcana into modern scenes in everyday situations that leave behind the medieval allegory of some cards.

What can I ask Tarot about?

Like almost everyone who has learned to read Tarot in the twenty-first century, we use it as a therapeutic tool, not a predictive one. Thanks to the contribution of psychology to Tarot interpretation throughout the twentieth century, it is hard to ignore the notion of archetypes and their impact on the collective unconscious as outlined by scholars like Sallie Nichols, based on Carl Jung's works. This approach associates Tarot arcana with archetypes – universal images or patterns that pre-exist in our human minds. Such archetypes appear in myths from the most diverse regions and times in history, as well as in art, dreams and literature, and include examples such as the Mother, the Fool and Evil.

This approach suggests that rather than focusing on future results, it is more interesting and useful to ask the Tarot about available energy, how we are likely to behave in the face of certain events, and the how and why of our inner processes. Of course, there is a style of Tarot reading that's predictive and offers more precise answers to our questions, but let's just say that those answers are nothing more than hypothesis with a certain chance of coming true. Neither the cards nor your Tarot reader knows if you'll finish your studies or get back together with your ex. Instead of a hypothetical prediction of what will happen, a Tarot reading could show you an image of your attitude in the face of continued studies or finding a new partner.

I always remember a somewhat awful experience I had when I got a card reading from a "witch" in a park in Buenos Aires. I asked a question regarding my relationship with my business partner. The Devil came up, and the woman warned me about imminent fraud. My partner and I have been working together for over ten years, our publishing house hasn't stopped growing ever since, and everything we do is equally inspiring and fruitful for both of us. I believe the fifteenth arcanum speaks of the passion and ambition we devote to our business, and the fact that we see each day as a victory. Our relationship is totally Capricorn in style, and every meeting contributes to building the creative "empire" that we dream of. As we both carry our fire as a flag, I think it's only natural to have faced some disagreements, as both of us try to impose our individual will. Sometimes the air has been a bit tense. But we have never broken apart, and I have never ever experienced anything remotely resembling fraud. As we will see later on, the archetype of the Devil is far deeper and more complex than foreseeing a hoax.

Below, you'll see some examples of how we can turn those questions requiring a "divination" reply into others that allow for an analysis of the situation and let us see ourselves reflected in the archetype of each arcanum.

A question looking for a predictive answer	A question for evolutive Tarot
What will my exam results be?	Why can't I focus on studying? Why am I blocked in this subject? What is my bond with this course?
How well will I do in love? Should I get together with my ex?	What is my energetic attitude toward love? Why am I not satisfied with my present situation? What is Tarot's advice on self-love? What is my relationship with freedom?
Will I travel this year?	What kind of energies await me on this trip? What else do I need to attend to before taking a trip? What might I learn from this trip?
Should I start a business?	What is the energy of my current job? What paths will open up if I start up a business? What is Tarot's advice about starting my own business?

To finish, I'd like to give you a piece of advice that's really useful to fight eagerness when we look for a quick, concrete reply from Tarot. The Argentine writer Jorge Luis Borges said: "Doubt is one of intelligence's names." I always turn to that phrase to explain that it's okay to feel confused and have many further questions after a Tarot reading. It is wiser to have existential questions than to believe we know the answers to everything. Nobody likes being told what to do. So why do we expect the cards to tell us where to go?

How do I shuffle and cut the deck?

In order to do a card reading, it's important to be focused. I recommend taking some deep breaths before shuffling, and preparing your body and the environment to be focused on the present. You can shuffle the cards in your own way, the way that is easiest for you. If you are doing the reading for someone else, let them shuffle the cards for a while as well, so that they can pass on their energy to the reading through their hands. Once you have both shuffled the cards, cut the deck into two or three parts, place them on the table, then gather them up again. Spread out the cards, forming a range and, before picking each card, try and look inside yourself. Some people advise cutting with your left hand, as it is less governed by reason. My suggestion is that you follow your instinct. Sometimes, it's interesting to spy on the last card, the one that is hiding in the middle of the deck, when you cut it into two piles.

It is important to note that, in online readings – which are more common since the Covid pandemic – the client won't be able to touch the cards. If that's the case, it is a good idea to start picking cards while they tell you their story, as a way of setting energy into motion. Another way of helping the client to come into contact with the cards that are coming out is to ask them to tell you a number (from 1 to 22 if you're working with the major arcana). The idea is that, after shuffling and cutting, instead of spreading out a range of cards facing down, you can place them on the table one by one until you reach the number chosen by the person. The last card you put down will be the first card of your reading.

Are there positive and negative cards?

Death does not speak of literal death, The Tower has a lot to teach us and The Lovers does not speak about romantic love. In the same way, cards that may appear gentle, like The Magician, The Chariot or The Star, hide their secrets. The 78 cards in the deck, with their mysterious and inevitable energies, have both a more active and a more dormant meaning, which I will call "reverse meaning" from now on. I always say that, when you get a card, you get both its pros and its cons. The reverse meaning of a card may come up simply as a warning, or it may not even manifest in your life after the question you asked.

What you should know is that the dark side of a card is always there, dormant, and sometimes it is not as far from the bright side as you might believe. For example, every time I speak about The Hanged Man, I appreciate its ability to rest, to stay calm and to remain unshakeable in its stillness. However, on its dark side, this card warns about a kind of passiveness that may mean procrastination, laziness or lack of responsibility. When do we move from being relaxed to being neglectful? For example, we may all agree on the fact that when the alarm clock goes off at 7 a.m. and we jump out of bed we are full of proactive vibes, quite the opposite of The Hanged Man. If the alarm clock goes off at 8 a.m., many people may think, "That's someone who has had a good night's sleep." But if it goes off at 10 a.m., almost everyone would think it had better be a weekend or a holiday for it to make sense in adult life. When do we move from appreciating the twelfth arcanum to frowning upon it? What's the boundary between good rest and despicable laziness? Who decides on that?

In order to be an emphatic Tarot reader, it is very important to bear in mind that it is not good to focus on absolutes. It is advisable to lower one's guard, let go of mental models and open up to the multiple layers of meaning that a card can offer. Let's remember that, in Tarot, as in life, almost everything is relative and depends on how we look at it.

What happens when a card is upside down?

As you are not using the Tarot pack for divination, before a reading you should make sure the cards are all in the upright position. This does not mean, however, that every card should be read as a positive. As mentioned previously, it depends. The context is set by the person who is looking for answers, as well as the other cards that come up. For example, The Magician foretells beginnings. Next to the Ace of Pentacles and The Emperor, this may suggest that something is coming together. On the other hand, surrounded by The Devil and the Seven of Swords, The Magician may warn of excessive ambition, theft of ideas or something being cut short. If the client tells us they are going through a crisis with their friends and we see The Empress, we won't be able to give them the traditional advice to enjoy life, because we know they are going through a rough time. In this particular context, The Empress may speak more of the idea of forgiving ourselves for our mistakes than going out and charming the world.

If a Tarot reading was always positive when the cards appear upright and negative when they are upside down, Tarot would be something rigid, almost mathematical. Far from that, Tarot reading is an art requiring the intelligence to remember the meaning of the cards, the intuition to channel new messages as they come and the openness to articulate all your knowledge in the context of the situation presented by the client. Did you think it was going to be easy? Mastering this practice takes time.

How do I cleanse the deck?

Sometimes, after using the deck a lot, you may feel it is a bit "charged". As with any energy exchange, the deck needs a moment to rest and to cleanse. In order to do this, most people smoke the deck with herbs or incense, letting the smoke go above and below the deck, moving the cards through the smoke and spreading them out in a fan so that the smoke cleans them out. Other people might use a crystal and leave the deck on their altar or in a special corner with the stone facing up, offering its energetic flow. Another very Virgo-style form of resetting the deck is by ordering it in the archetypal hero path order. I encourage you to find your own way of cleansing your cards. And, if you feel like being literal and using a damp cloth to clean them from time to time, that's okay too.

How do I find my life arcanum?

In order to find out what your life arcanum is, add up the figures in your date of birth, one by one. For example, if you were born on 24 April 1994, your card will come from adding up:

$$2 + 4 + 0 + 4 + 1 + 9 + 9 + 4 = 33$$

As 33 is higher than the number of the major arcana, you will have to reduce it to a number between 1 and 22, like this:

$$3 + 3 = 6$$

The sixth arcanum is The Lovers. This represents the energy you came into the world with. You can find out about the characteristics of this arcanum and see which of them you resonate with and which you don't. The bad news is that many people resist their life arcanum at the beginning. The good news is they always end up liking it. It is useful to see how the qualities and challenges of the arcanum find new meaning in the different stages in your life. It can also be useful to calculate the cards of your friends and use your knowledge about them to complement your insight about each card.

How do I find my year arcanum?

If you want to know which card represents a certain year in your life, you need to add up the numbers in your birthday in that year. Taking the previous example, let's calculate which card was with you during 2020:

$$2 + 4 + 0 + 4 + 2 + 0 + 2 + 0 = 14$$

Temperance is the fourteenth arcanum. With this arcanum as the archetype of the year, I would wonder about patience, consolidating processes, everything you've been able to bring together and what is left to do.

Numerology in Tarot

Knowing the meaning of numbers is a simple and valuable tool in Tarot. When you don't remember the exact meaning of a card, paying attention to its number can help you out. But, even if you know the deck thoroughly, the numbers provide fundamental information. It's important to note that numerology, the understanding of the meaning of individual numbers in Tarot, is different from the use of numbers to carry out mathematical calculations, such as the one used to work out our arcanum based on our date of birth.

In Tarot, odd numbers refer to an active attitude. As I once heard: "They like the future", and with their explosive energy they have the ability to fit the present moment and set the tone. They are action numbers that won't go unnoticed. On the other hand, even numbers are defined by their receptive attitude. They feel more comfortable "looking at the past", and have a slower rhythm, focusing on looking inside yourself, remaining still and being receptive to the available energy.

The 22 major arcana, the minor arcana and the court cards can also be assigned different degrees, from one to ten. The degree of most cards is determined by its ending number. For example, The Chariot is seven and therefore belongs to the seventh degree. The Star is 17 and also belongs to the seventh degree, together with the seventh card of each suit in the minor arcana: Seven of Wands, Seven of Swords, Seven of Cups and Seven of Pentacles. Note that, within this ranking, The Fool (number zero) is assigned to the first degree, together with The Magician and Strength, given its qualities of initiation or beginning. The World (number 21) – even though it does not end in zero – is considered within the tenth degree, together with Wheel of Fortune and Judgement, because of its qualities of ending or closure.

The following image shows the ten degrees in numerology, their characteristics and the major arcana that belong to each degree.

In order to see this ranking of the major arcana in ten degrees, I invite you to pay attention to nature. You will see that life cycles unfold in an organic process that is organized in the same degrees. For example, let's look at the example of a lemon tree.

First degree:

Seeds are planted. The intention is to begin. There is plenty of potential but little experience, as represented by The Fool (0), The Magician (I) or Strength (XI).

Second degree:

Roots grow. The process is hidden, and we may become a little uneasy, as we cannot yet see any results, as happens with The High Priestess (II) and The Hanged Man (XII).

Third degree:

The first shoot appears and everything sparkles. The plant has expressed itself – it has germinated and wants to grow. This explosion is experienced like The Empress (III) and Death (XIII).

Fourth degree:

The stalk grows, a structure that will offer the plant the solid support it needs to develop, as in The Emperor (IV) and Temperance (XIV).

Fifth degree:

Leaves offer the social dynamics represented by The Hierophant (V) and The Devil (XV). These cards ask us to consider whether those around us are mates, masters or competitors.

Sixth degree:

Buds appear, reminding us of the idea of beauty and contemplation, as in The Lovers (VI) and The Tower (XVI). The Tower invites us to jump off the oppressive structure and seek that beauty.

Seventh degree:

Fruit appears – in this case a lemon – and we experience success, as in The Chariot (VII) and The Star (XVII).

Eighth degree:

Adjustment takes place and at the exact moment of maturity fruit is ready to collect. After the progress represented in The Chariot, we fix our course. This accuracy and intuition are offered by Justice (VIII) and The Moon (XVIII).

Ninth degree:

The fruit spoils and turns brown because we haven't collected it. At this point The Hermit (IX) is in crisis and searches for truth, The Sun (XIX) finds the answers and shares it with the world.

Tenth degree:

The cycle ends, and the fruit may fall from the plant and rot or become compost to fertilize the soil. The type of ending will depend on the different arcana: Wheel of Fortune (X), Judgement (XX) or The World (XXI).

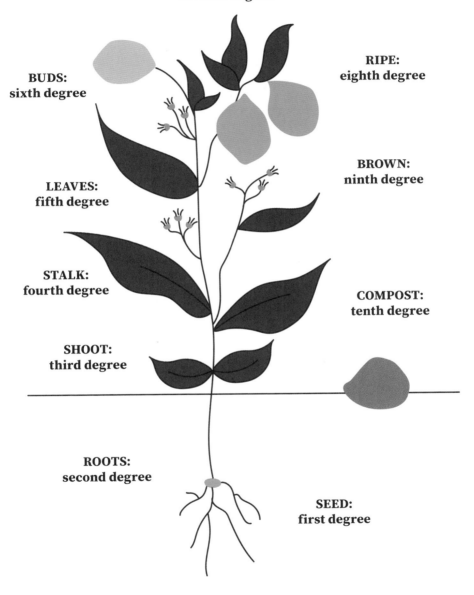

FRUIT:
seventh degree

RIPE:
eighth degree

BUDS:
sixth degree

BROWN:
ninth degree

LEAVES:
fifth degree

STALK:
fourth degree

COMPOST:
tenth degree

SHOOT:
third degree

ROOTS:
second degree

SEED:
first degree

MAJOR ARCANA

Arcane (*adjective*)

1. Known or knowable only to a few people; secret.
2. Broadly: mysterious, obscure.

Arcanum (*noun*)

Mysterious or specialized knowledge, language or information accessible or possessed only by one who knows the secrets.

The 22 major arcana are the essential cards in Tarot. Each one represents an archetypal energy, relating to an ideal model that lives in our collective subconscious. For example, the idea of initiating, realizing or ending something is not expressed in exactly the same way for every person, but there is an underlying connection between the different ways in which these facts manifest. **As each major arcanum condenses the energy of an archetype, you will inevitably identify with these images at different points throughout your life.**

You may generally feel closer to certain cards than others, but allow yourself to remain open to change and new energies as this can be very revealing. You'll have seen in the definition above that an arcanum is a secret, and you are about to find out about the major secrets in the deck.

As you read about the cards, observe the direction in which the characters look and the position of their body. Understanding a card is not about learning its definition by heart. It is about identifying its hidden message and interpreting this with your own mind. The gestures, poses and colours in the cards may communicate more than my words.

THE FOOL

THE FOOL

Not all those who wander are lost.

J. R. R. Tolkien

Vital drive

The Fool is the arcanum that sets the Tarot in motion. It is pure, contained energy and, when this card is drawn in a reading, it works as a powerful magnet, capable of bringing us back from a mysterious point in the universe. As the arcanum that starts the deck, it is usually said to be the card **with the greatest potential, but no experience whatsoever.** It is precisely that potential that leads us to set ourselves into motion and can take us out of our comfort zone. The Fool's way of moving forward is with the rhythm of music, naked and with no predetermined destination. However, just because he is wandering does not mean that he is lost.

As is the case with any new start, The Fool is usually untidy, unstructured and less focused on the rules. Let us say he is not authority's best friend. Throughout the journey, he will be willing to make friends, though in the beginning he may look mostly inwards.

The card

Having no number, this card plays as a joker. In some decks, it is considered as zero and in others as 22, because it also has the energy to move on after the twenty-first arcanum. The Fool has the power to bring The World back from the clouds. As a symbol of his austerity he carries very little luggage and he's so free he seems to ignore the dog following him. Some say the dog is precisely what pushes him forward. Others see it as just a companion.

The Fool in a reading about love

This card represents inexplicable magnetism. **As an eternal traveller, The Fool brings about the spontaneity that is needed for any adventure.** Mind you, The Fool does not like contracts or attachments of any kind. The Fool's freedom runs both ways: he can return as freely as he once left. Anything is possible with this character.

Reversed meaning

Dispersing, disruptive, solitary. In reverse, this card may express elusiveness, and it may warn about someone who is not emotionally responsible. **When he runs away, The Fool hurts others. When he gets lost, he neglects himself.** This path of irresponsibility leads nowhere. A stuck Fool can represent a huge loss of energy.

Advice

Forget about form. Enter a trance and **return to original madness.** There are no reasons. Just act.

In a reading

Often, **The Fool leads the way and invites us to take risks.** Before a card, The Fool passes its creative power on to that card. In the final position, it represents liberation, running away or a reduction in energy. The question is: where is the energy going?

Astrological correspondence

Traditionally, The Fool is considered to be made of Air (the element in Gemini, Libra and Aquarius): light, quick and vital, and so necessary for life sometimes. It's the breath of fresh air we need when we are overwhelmed, although there may also be traits of an Aquarius Moon, with its entirely unattached energy, finding refuge in diversity and being attracted to eclectic things.

A curious fact that helped me understand this card

>•>•>•>•>•>•>>•>•>•>•>•>>•>•>•>•>•>>•>•>•>•>>•>•>•>•>•>>•>

The first Tarot deck I had was a golden, very bright version of the classic Rider–Waite–Smith deck. When I found out it had been illustrated by a woman, Pamela Colman Smith, I became obsessed with knowing the details of her story. Waite participated in the design of the major arcana, but Colman Smith had more freedom to work with the minor arcana. Unfortunately, she was paid very little for her work and she died in poverty. Another interesting piece of information is that the image of The Fool resembles the character of Peter Pan. That's no coincidence. Colman Smith had been commissioned to illustrate a children's version of *The Boy who Wouldn't Grow Up*, a publication by the Scottish James M. Barrie, during the time she was working with the deck. Some of that innocence and naughtiness is seen in her version of The Fool.

Living the energy of The Fool

Go out to the street. Now. Wearing whatever you are wearing. Get up from your chair and start moving. Take a walk around the block. If you feel like going further, why not? You may end up window shopping, visiting a friend or at the door of a museum. Just don't decide where you are going before you set off. Don't take too much money or too many things with you, only the essentials. The Fool invites you to wander the streets in your neighbourhood and watch everything as if you were seeing it for the first time. Liberate yourself from aims and possessions, and roam around freely.

THE FOOL

THE MAGICIAN

I. THE MAGICIAN

Every truth has the structure of fiction.

Jacques Lacan

Initiator

If The Fool is considered the origin of Tarot, The Magician represents the beginning. He is the one who comes up with the plan. He can start the game because he knows his chances. **Instead of wandering around, The Magician settles down somewhere, defines a position at the table and shows his elements. Having everything in sight and at hand, he can then choose his next move.** This is a beginning that requires courage, not mastery. The Magician is the typical *maker*, a great craftsman. He is full of mental activity and, if anything, is sometimes too imaginative. He will excel thanks to his ideas and other arcana will carry them out.

The card

A young man is behind a table with the four suits in sight: wands, swords, cups and pentacles. In most decks, the table is seen from such an angle that one of its legs is not visible. This poses a question about support. Is the table stable? The character conceals a snide smile and is looking out of the corner of his eye. He is hiding something. What is he capable of? The symbol of infinity in this card means this man, though young, is determined to go far. His belt is a symbol of willpower.

The Magician in a reading about love

This card means there is a connection. **In a reading about love, it may mean a relationship that is growing from interesting conversations and laughter.** The card can hint at immaturity in the other person, but sometimes this teenage spirit can be attractive.

Reversed meaning

What's the reversed meaning of the great spectacle offered by The Magician? We are faced with a character who will find a way to convince us at all costs. The main risk of this arcanum is that it may be hiding a lie among promising words. The Magician may act as a classic conman.

Advice

Start. The worst mistake is to keep waiting for the right moment. There is no such moment. This card reminds you that you already have the resources. Use them without revealing your secret.

In a reading

Regardless of whether this card shows its alchemist version (a creator of matter and projects) or illusionist (saying seductive things in order to achieve his goal), The Magician always advises to **pay attention to the elements at our disposal to start our project**.

Astrological correspondence

The Magician is associated with Mercury, the planet of communication, exchange and reasoning. Wherever this planet is in your natal chart, it will indicate what you are interested in learning or understanding, and the wisdom you want to seek.

A curious fact that helped me understand this card

>•>

The surrealist artist Salvador Dalí created a Tarot deck and painted himself as The Magician. Portraying himself next to his worktable, Dalí shows us that magic is not seen as something supernatural, but is what happens when we discover and use our talent. In fact, on his Tarot table, Dalí drew a melting clock, as is typical of his style. This is a symbol of the elasticity of our personal time. It is never too late to open up to those ideas that make us unique. It is never too late to begin.

Living the energy of The Magician

Add something of the essential energy of The Magician to your life. What you know is enough. If you don't know anything, look at the card. You know what The Fool is about. Learn to be ingenious. If you express yourself with confidence, people will believe you.

THE HIGH PRIESTESS

II. THE HIGH PRIESTESS

A well-read woman is a dangerous creature.

Lisa Kleypas

Inner world

Every process has a gestational period when nothing seems to happen. But the truth is that, like a recently planted tree growing roots, we need time to accumulate energy on the inside. It is the time when a project is developing. **This moment requires perseverance, patience, faith and a good dose of self-knowledge.** The High Priestess is the first woman to appear in the Tarot deck. This may represent the first fight in the history of feminism: the fight to access knowledge.

The legend of the High Priestess Juana tells the story of a woman in the ninth century who decided to disguise herself as a man, with her mother's help, in order to be able to study. She ended up being a scholar, a well-known teacher, an expert on religion and ultimately the Pope. All this she did disguised as a man. Apparently, the ploy ended when people found out she was pregnant. Ouch!

The card

Being an even number, the energy of this card is receptive. This means it reminds us we need moments of stillness and contemplation to receive all the knowledge the universe has for us. The High Priestess represents the mother or grandmother archetype. The card shows a seated woman covered by several layers of clothing. Behind her, a tapestry separates her from the rest of the world. All these elements are symbols of the woman's secrecy and self-preservation. She is holding a book, a symbol of the wisdom surrounding this arcanum. The white egg she's carrying around her neck means something fertile is growing inside.

The High Priestess in a reading about love

I would say this card tells you to be cautious for now. You are intuitive, assertive and full of knowledge. Maybe you should ask yourself this question: **How can I connect to somebody else when I am so protective of myself?** If The High Priestess appears in a reading with other cards foretelling sharing energy, such as The Sun or The Emperor, it may mean that bonds are being woven from the roots.

Reversed meaning

Inflexible, dogmatic and cold. In her shadowy aspects, The High Priestess is comparable to Bernarda Alba, from Federico García Lorca's play *The House of Bernarda Alba*, for whom **morality is more important than feelings.** This matriarch is obsessed with chastity and rejects any connection to body and desire, which begins a vicious circle that affects her whole family's life.

Advice

You should see beyond the obvious, be patient and wait for the process to unfold. Focus on yourself, preserve yourself, respect yourself. **Being alone does not mean being lonely**. It's about learning how to be with yourself. The psychoanalyst Carl Jung said: "Who looks outside, dreams; who looks inside, awakes."

In a reading

It's not time for concrete and visible results. The question is: **what's going on inside?** This may be a moment of purification, vibrating with nature, loving ourselves, writing to heal.

Astrological correspondence

The High Priestess is linked to the energy of The Moon. This card is associated with the ability to feel affection, and those things that touch you and nurture your soul. It draws attention to the things that you fear and the places where you choose to take shelter.

A curious fact that helped me understand this card

In her book *How to Suppress Women's Writing,* Joanna Russ exposes and comments on ten ways in which literary criticism has ignored, condemned or underestimated women's writing. Virginia Woolf denounces something similar in her essay *A Room of One's Own.* What were women doing until the early twentieth century, only having written 5 per cent (or less) of the books found in a library? The few who were published (Mary Shelley, the Brontë sisters and Emily Dickinson, among others) were considered geniuses, with exceptional qualities for their gender, which suppressed any chance of a female literary tradition. Directly or indirectly, this has led to an exclusion of women from the canon. The High Priestess, holding nothing less than a book, reminds us that women have been writing for centuries, even with few role models, publishing under male pen names and without a room of their own.

Living the energy of The High Priestess

Which book made you a reader? It may be one from your childhood. The book your parents read to you, or a book that spoke to you at school. Find the book among your old possessions. If you can't do that, find it online. How does it make you feel? What part of you comes back to life with those words? Remember that something of what led you to that book is still alive inside you.

THE EMPRESS

III. THE EMPRESS

Imperfect action beats perfect inaction.

Harry S. Truman

. . . .

Energetic eruption

If The Magician is the seed of a plant that we are giving life to and The High Priestess represents the moment its roots grow, then The Empress is the manifestation of the first shoot. There is not a lot of previous experience or a pre-defined shape in this first growth. There's only presence. She says: "Here I am." And, of course, everything around her is set into motion thanks to the energy of the plant germinating. **When we get very excited about something, we feel like teenagers again.** Fertility, curiosity and creativity take hold, and we feel we can do anything. It's always springtime for The Empress – a hormonal spring that shows its feelings.

Interestingly, when we compare this card to The High Priestess, we can see that the differences in the images indicate different attitudes toward life. While the second arcanum inhabits and explores the inner world, The Empress is empowered and comes into contact with the outer world. In fact, she plays a crucial role in that outside world. Her attitude is: "I attract everything I wish for."

The card

This seated woman is visibly younger and more carefree than The High Priestess. Her legs are relaxed and she's wearing less clothing. She looks toward the future and carries a sceptre that touches her navel, as if she is saying: "I do what I want." We can also see an Adam's apple on her throat. Some scholars claim that this represents her "masculine" active attitude. This character will often get into trouble by saying something inappropriate at the wrong time or in the wrong place.

The Empress in a reading about love

This woman takes control and deals with things. **She's so excitable she cannot always see how real her feelings are.** Clumsy and fanatical, she likes to attract attention, but she always has fun. In a reading about love, The Empress means the encounter will be free and fiery or it won't happen at all.

Reversed meaning

When instinct dominates your actions, you end up aimless. **If everything is on the outside, you risk neglecting your inner world.** Jealousy. In its shadowy aspect, The Empress speaks of someone who is arrogant, too daring, a bit manipulative or has a lazy attitude toward life: "Let everybody come to me."

Advice

Activate your desire. Explore. You are creative fire. **Don't think about the results; just enjoy yourself.** Expose yourself, come out, love yourself. Say "yes" to chaos.

In a reading

A sudden start may have consequences. At first, this fertile transformation can attract powerful desire, but in its "warning" mode, this card reminds you that less mature actions will have consequences. **The good news is The Empress does not punish herself.** Luckily for you, in her freshness and lightness, she is very self-indulgent.

Astrological correspondence

The Empress is associated with Venus. She represents everything you cherish, and your capacity to love, to choose and to share with others. The question brought about by this planet is: what do you like about yourself and what do you like about others? Identifying this is the first step toward attracting these qualities to yourself.

A curious fact that helped me understand this card

>•>•>•>•>•>>•>•>•>•>•>>•>•>•>•>•>>•>•>•>•>•>>•>•>•>•>•>>•>•>

Back to the Tarot deck painted by Salvador Dalí: for this card, he chose to paint the face of his wife, Gala. She was crucial to Dalí's career. So much so, that he even signed some of his paintings as Gala Salvador Dalí. She was a woman with an overwhelming sex drive and she made all the couple's decisions, from the most trivial to the most important. Gala also read Tarot.

Living the energy of The Empress

Make a list of the things you like doing and that represent you. Identify if these are things you liked as a child, or if you discovered them as you grew up. How long has it been since you last found time to do them? Take a break, make a date with yourself and start enjoying.

THE EMPEROR

IV. THE EMPEROR

I believe in what I see.

Mastering practice

The Emperor is here to solve any problems The Empress may have with sustaining attention. The Emperor takes care of this, as the trunk or stem of the project. He offers discipline, stability and the effort required to master something or achieve material goals. In Tarot, when we talk about material things, we don't only mean money. We mean routines, family structures, time, the body and everything we need to organize ourselves socially. **The Emperor brings about the energy of stability.** He represents the four legs of a chair that allow us to sit, knowing we won't fall. He is the ground and ceiling of the house where we were born. He is authority; he regulates and protects us. The Emperor may seem boring, but he is vital. Without his certainty, it would be impossible to even think about creating.

The card

A man is sitting on his throne, proud of what he's conquered and ready to take action. He wears the belt of willpower. He stares at the object he wants to protect and master. He is in control of what he knows, which also means that he is not so open to new things. He holds his sceptre in an upright position, as a symbol of his objectivity and rationality.

The Emperor in a reading about love

Being a providing and rational character, The Emperor was historically associated with the archetype of the father. Nowadays, the associations are with structure, decision-making and power. **The Emperor may suggest the presence of a stable partner who is part of a cosy home.** But beware looking for someone who is too similar to a father figure; you may end up with a person who is inflexible and wants to dominate the relationship.

Reversed meaning

The Emperor also indicates the dark side of power. He can become arrogant, authoritarian and despotic. **Either consciously or subconsciously, The Emperor is constantly telling us what to do and he sets rigid boundaries.** This can indicate narrow mindedness and something that is out of date rather than classic. Remember, it is one thing to put down strong roots and a very different thing to be stuck somewhere forever.

Advice

It is time to lay down foundations, settle down and build. **It is time to organize the chaos left by The Empress.** This card offers peace of mind in exchange for constancy and effort.

In a reading

It's important to pay attention to the cards that surround The Emperor. In a conquering mood, The Emperor will drive us to win our own battles. He is a sound voice, offering support. In the final position, the card may mean boredom, the inability to connect to sensitivity or being fed up with having to decide.

Astrological correspondence

Associated with the sign of Aries, the astrological correspondence of The Emperor is probably the least convincing of the major arcana. Remember that these were the associations of the members of the Hermetic Order of the Golden Dawn, including Arthur Edward Waite and Aleister Crowley. A hundred years later, we can see the correspondence between Aries and The Emperor in the ability to start things positively, facing them head on. However, Aries is a spontaneous sign, tending toward chaos, while the fourth arcanum is highly structured and seeks to exercise his authority in a stable environment. This is similar to Saturn in Aries, or Aries in the tenth house. Such combinations give Aries the solid structure to match The Emperor.

A curious fact that helped me understand this card

During the process of writing this book, in 2018, I found out that the life arcanum of Josefina Schargorodsky, our illustrator, was The Emperor. Given Josefina's inclination to aesthetics, as well as her fertile creativity, I thought it was reasonable to associate her with The Empress, The Lovers or even The Star. But, as I looked closely, I could see The Emperor represented her in more profound ways. While drawing the illustrations for this book, she was pregnant with her first baby, though she didn't mention this and it didn't show at all. She drew all of the illustrations in 60 days during her second trimester, showing a great sense of responsibility and commitment to the project. Her mature attitude toward work made me understand that no creative person can succeed with talent alone; they also need a high degree of discipline. Josefina shows all of these qualities.

Living the energy of The Emperor

Have you ever wondered what the four legs of your chair are? Brainstorm about the potential pillars of your life. Discard those that lose strength in comparison to others. Keep four of them. Write them down somewhere visible. You are already supported by the four legs of your chair.

THE HIEROPHANT

V. THE HIEROPHANT

Faith does not make things easy; it makes things possible.

Luke 1: 37

A bridge to another dimension

The Hierophant is the first card that shows more than one person. This card opens up the group dimension, interactions and power relationships. The Hierophant is a master who will show us a world beyond what we know: a spiritual world to feed our interests. If Earth is what is real, and The Emperor helps us master earthly practices, the sky is where our dreams are projected. Our vocation may seem to be too far away, but it's not unattainable. **We should take a leap of faith and cross the bridge toward that new dimension.** The Hierophant is a guide showing us the way. His speech engages us. He gives us something to believe in.

The card

A pope is on his pulpit looking out of the corner of his eye. His audience is made up of people who believe him and praise him. We can see the communication between him and these people: the message, the channel, the sender, the receiver. Will he, the main speaker, let anybody else speak at any point? The mudra, the symbolic hand gesture, that the pope is using indicates we should move on. His fingers point at the future as if saying: "Once you've swum to the middle of the river, you cannot go back."

The Hierophant in a reading about love

In a reading about love, this card means there's a person playing the leading role. A master, a therapist, somebody from whom you learn and whom you usually idealize. **You see this person as your God on Earth.** Such fascination with somebody else's words may result in an asymmetrical relationship. In other cases, the card may mean a relationship will become formal.

Reversed meaning

In its negative aspect, The Hierophant shows the imposition of his religion, or his ideology, as the only possible worldview. **Fascination and secrets may lead to manipulation.** The other side of this card is the fifteenth arcanum, The Devil. The Hierophant may suggest a situation of power abuse, little empathy and deceit.

Advice

Dare to talk. **Leave your comfort zone behind and evolve in your art.** Don't believe you know it all. Look around. Finally, don't let seducing ideals deceive you.

In a reading

Pay attention, **the energy driving you may call you to learn something new.** This may mean studying, courses, spiritual trips, coming into contact with occult art. This card may also warn you about a risk: a scam, a con artist, someone selling you something without giving you the chance to check it out first. Which of these characters are you: the one who knows and commands or the one who listens and obeys?

Astrological correspondence

This arcanum is associated with Taurus. Being the first earth sign, this correspondence reminds us that the fifth arcanum is about bringing the most sublime beliefs to the earthly plane. Also, The Hierophant and the sign of Taurus share the focus on traditions, rules, sumptuous attire and the importance of symbol. Another thing leaders have in common with Taurus energy is that they usually live a life of comfort and pleasure. And, of course, they can be very stubborn.

If we revise the idea of moral authority as expressed by The Hierophant, we may also associate it with Saturn in Sagittarius: people who love to preach and seduce us with their ideas.

A curious fact that helped me understand this card

Sallie Nichols offers an interesting insight into this complex arcanum in her book *Jung and Tarot*, first published in 1980. Among other things, she reminds us that the Latin root of the word "pontiff" comes from *pontifex*: he who acts as a bridge. She also compares The Hierophant with The High Priestess consulting the law in her book. The Hierophant carries no book; he himself is the law. In fact, this archetype of leader and followers can be seen in influential figures of many causes such as veganism, ecology and feminism, and even in the contemporary figure of the social media influencer. The archetype of the Pope invites us to search for sense, and to belong to a group where we can both question and validate our beliefs.

Living the energy of The Hierophant

Make a collage about all your idols: rock stars, film stars, writers, artists, your mum, your dad, your best friend. Feel free to include anyone who comes to mind. Look for your most genuine source of inspiration.

THE LOVERS

VI. THE LOVERS

How do you choose without losing?

Triangulating decisions

Some say this card represents wasting energy while hesitating. However, we should see **that hesitation is a legitimate part of the process of choice,** and that we are always what we choose, even if we define ourselves by the choice we *didn't* make. As the Nobel poet Wislawa Szymborska said: "By choosing, I reject. There is no other method." The Lovers is similar to The Fool, only six steps later, when it's time to choose a path. The card has nothing to do with being in love, but with the **deep search for beauty or, as I like to put it, being in love with life.** The Lovers urge you to do what you like, but also confront you with uncertainty and choices between things that can be interpreted in different ways.

The card

A person of androgynous features, neither female nor male, struggles to choose between two options: one represents the new and offers to go forward; the other, representing the old, drags them backward. The characters' hands are all entwined and Cupid's arrow above them seems to whisper: "Let your heart choose."

The Lovers in a reading about love

Is someone hesitating? Is there a third person? Or is everything in your mind? This card calls for patience. It's okay to have more questions than answers.

Reversed meaning

When you lose sight of your values, you may end up adopting other people's values. That flexibility can draw you into conflicts that are not your own. **It's okay to hesitate.** The problem is not having doubts, but getting lost in the various different options and losing touch with yourself.

Advice

Follow your own desires. Is your environment too busy? Clear out the debris. Other people may be trying to influence your decisions. **Beware of the forces dragging you backward and those pulling you forward.** It's time to accept the grey areas. When nothing is certain, everything is possible.

In a reading

The Lovers means complexity. There are some questions you can ask yourself if this card comes up in a reading: **why don't you stop imagining what you would like to do and start doing it?** Are you held back by the past? What have you experienced so far that has led you to the things that you like? It's time to redefine your priorities: what's good and bad, what you let in and what you leave out. But, before that: why do you care so much about other people's opinions?

Astrological correspondence

This arcanum is associated with Gemini, the art of thinking without risks. This air sign represents many different interests and the desire to say yes to everything. Open to all the options, Gemini risks being distracted and without focus. This association to The Lovers is reflected in the proverb: He that too much embraceth, holds little.

A curious fact that helped me understand this card

>•>

Comparing the Marseilles and Rider–Waite–Smith Tarot decks, there is a substantial difference in the name of this card and the images on it. In the Marseilles deck, the card is called "The Lover" and it refers to a person who, in a state of infatuation and mental distraction, has to choose between two options. In the Rider–Waite–Smith deck, the card is called "The Lovers" and the image shows a naked couple, probably alluding to Adam and Eve, and the idea of experiencing deep, irresistible connection. At first, everything seems to flourish, but then we remember that, in Roman mythology, the gods were afraid of Cupid as he could ruin your life with one shot of his arrow. When something touches your heart, whether it is to do with work or relationships, you should take responsibility.

Living the energy of The Lovers

Make your own playlist. Choose the criteria for the list – studying, training or raising your spirits – and then carefully select at least 20 songs that relate to that inspiration.

VII. THE CHARIOT

I travel, therefore I am.

Action in the world

Seven is a lucky number in many cultures. There are seven chakras, the moon phase changes every seven days, a week is made up of seven days, there are seven wonders in the world. **In order to inhabit the energy of The Chariot, you have to know where it's heading.** This is an effortless movement. Things work out because they drive you forward, or you've found your place. In fact, if you chose wisely in the previous card, The Lovers, things will flow better in this one. Otherwise, you may cover thousands of miles in a direction that is not ideal for you. This card is said to represent the aspirational horizon of humans on Earth. It's what we know as success in today's world.

The card

A luxurious chariot is pulled by two horses. In what direction are they looking? Are they moving or simply posing? The driver is young. Is he the owner of the chariot or has he borrowed it to make it look as if it's his? The masks he carries on his shoulders may mean that, in order to move toward certain places, you need to hide some part of yourself.

The Chariot in a reading about love

The lover is brave and the meeting is invigorating. **There's no doubt you will be able to move forward with this person.** You just have to check that the direction is the right one. And, beware! If you can go forward, remember that you can go backward at the same speed.

Reversed meaning

Narcissistic and vain, the driver of The Chariot may be pretending to move, faking success, because he knows there are many eyes on him. **So, he makes himself comfortable and seeks applause,** but he does not make an effort to be true to himself or enjoy the journey. Another possible reading of The Chariot is that progress is so fast there is no time to keep a record of what is going on.

Advice

Don't stop. Take action. It will happen. **The only way to get ahead is to get started.** Make sure your horses are aligned, and that this is a movement toward personal development and not just a spectacle for others to see.

In a reading

Energy moves clearly in a particular direction. This card foretells trips. On the one hand, it suggests moving pieces, a victory or finding your inner magic. On the other hand, the card questions who the chariot belongs to. It may signify recklessness, or going faster than you can control.

Astrological correspondence

This arcanum is associated with Cancer, a water sign represented by the crab: being protected by your own self and carrying your home with you. The Chariot can be in constant motion and therefore knows how to make a home everywhere it goes. Both the card and the sign also refer to the idea of overcoming obstacles.

A curious fact that helped me understand this card

>•>

I had been in the Tarot world for a short time when I met Sara Amor, a Brazilian transgender artist living in Buenos Aires. Amor had illustrated her own truly beautiful, original Tarot deck, that is full of intertextuality. In her deck, called "The Machine", the seventh arcanum is an overturned chariot. Smoke is coming out of it after a crash and it is probably a police car, as two police officers are walking next to it. In this deck, The Chariot warns you about how things can go wrong if you search for excessive success at too great a speed.

Living the energy of The Chariot

Think of all the things you always say you will do but never achieve. Rank them in order of importance and set a deadline for each one. Write down in detail everything you need to do to achieve each goal. Then, close your eyes and picture yourself doing all those things successfully, step by step. See yourself succeeding. Experience the taste of success. You've made it. In your mind, success is guaranteed. Now you are ready to make things come true.

VIII

JUSTICE

VIII. JUSTICE

Karma is not a bitch. It's a mirror.

Laurie Lynn

Balance

In The Lovers, life presents you with the idea of choosing something, hopefully something that aligns with your own personal taste and connects with your vocation. Then, The Chariot pushes you forward in that direction. Justice invites you to make corrections to that progress. Let's say that, in the sixth arcanum, you realize you want to be a poet. The seventh arcanum makes you publish a book. In the eighth arcanum, you want to make a lot of changes to the book and do not let anybody read it until the second revised edition is published. Perfection does not exist. However, you want to come close to it. That is what Justice encourages: a state of excellence. Morality, severity and honour are qualities of Justice, much like those of a very strict mother.

The card

A woman is carrying a sword in one hand and a set of scales in the other – balancing and adjusting. When things go too far, you need to cut your losses. If you are wrong, take responsibility. This woman does not flinch. She has a third eye and her outfit is heavy. She may seem rigid, but she is stable: number eight is two times four.

Justice in a reading about love

Love in unequal conditions is not love. This card encourages you to wake up from your fantasy. **Justice is not characterized by being carried away; instead, she considers what's in her best interest.** She consents to and believes in commitment.

Reversed meaning

High expectations bring with them the possibility of disappointment. In reverse, this card may represent somebody who is dogmatic and inflexible. **It may suggest a situation in which things are banned or need to be authorized.** When stuck, this card represents the bureaucracy that blocks freedom.

Advice

Respect yourself. Give yourself what you deserve. **Can you separate the wheat from the chaff and reject those things that don't help you?** Or wake up and smell the coffee: your problems are your own to deal with.

In a reading

It's time to put everything in its right place. Will you give or take? **Ask yourself if you are setting the right boundaries. What is the role you play and what is your responsibility?**

Astrological correspondence

Libra is an air sign symbolizing balance. It has aesthetic energy. It is kind and diplomatic. There's a certain neatness in not taking sides and that is morally right, as suggested by the Justice card.

A curious fact that helped me understand this card

In the Thoth Tarot deck, created by the occultist Aleister Crowley and illustrated by Frieda Harris, Justice is called Adjustment. The card shows a cold, sharp and inflexible image, referring to the adjustments made by nature in order to keep things balanced. In the letters exchanged with Harris in 1939, Crowley harshly criticized her first vision of Justice. She replied: "I will also do a new Justice, damn her. Do you think there was ever, 'a woman satisfied'?"

Living the energy of Justice

Over the course of a week, count all the times you say "yes" when you mean "no". Does the result surprise you? Think about what you could do in order to be more faithful to your own wishes. What could you do in order to reduce that number?

IX

THE HERMIT

IX. THE HERMIT

*Going to another country doesn't make any difference.
I've tried all that. You can't get away from yourself
by moving from one place to another. There's nothing
to that.*

Ernest Hemingway

Crisis

We let go of the perfection proposed by Justice to search for the truth. We surrender to the crisis that is inevitable after a long journey, especially after the distance travelled by The Chariot. We are far from home and it is time to look inside ourselves. The answers are to be found in our past. We retreat from the world to make a personal quest for light. Being a hermit does not mean staying in on Friday evening watching TV. **It means increasing the distance between us and the world, and isolating ourselves in order to reflect.** The hermit proposes the deepest search inside ourselves. We can be confident that he will always lead us to be more genuine.

The card

An old man walks down a dark path, turning his back to the world. He is wearing many layers of clothing and a heavy coat. The card has an odd number, which means this man will be active in his search.

The Hermit in a reading about love

In the quest for love, you may find yourself. **You may find somebody who is going through a profound process of personal change.** Join that search with humility; that person who is exploring their inner world is bound to have something to teach you.

Reversed meaning

Avoiding problems does not help. **Nor does resisting change, dismissing your own sensitivities or ignoring the past.** The reverse meaning is not the opposite of a hermit; it is not a sociable person. On the contrary, the negative side of this card represents somebody who refuses to look inside themselves.

Advice

The search is inwards and in solitude. **What lightens your path?** Nobody knows what the future holds. Walk through uncertainty with bravery.

In a reading

If this card appears between two others, The Hermit will be turning his back to one of them and mildly illuminating the other one. Think about this: what do you ignore about yourself? Relax. It may be time to turn your back on certain plans. On the other hand, ask yourself what is right in front of you that you can't see. Being the second earth sign in the zodiac, Virgo is focused on the details and wanting everything to work perfectly. The phrase that represents this is: "The house has the right to show affection." Before sharing their knowledge with the world, Virgos need to look inside themselves, in the same way as the ninth arcanum.

A curious fact that helped me understand this card

>•>•>•>•>•>•>•>•>•>•>•>•>•>>•>•>•>•>•>•>>•>•>•>•>•>•>•>>•>•>•>•>•>•>•>

There is a contemporary Tarot deck called "Spirit of Our Time". It was created by Israeli artist Tao-B. The Hermit of this deck shows a young man standing on the subway, absorbed in his mobile phone and with his headphones on. Two older ladies are sitting next to him, but he doesn't seem to take any notice of them or of his surroundings. This makes me wonder what happens to empathy when we decide to close ourselves off from the rest of the world. Is it necessary to interact with people all the time? Will we know how to get out of this state of self-absorption when someone near us needs help?

Living the energy of The Hermit

If you had to describe yourself through somebody else's eyes – for example, your friend's eyes – what would you say? What would you point out as your strengths and weaknesses? Look at yourself in the mirror and speak to yourself as if you were your closest friend, one who looks at you with tenderness. What is your friend's advice?

WHEEL OF FORTUNE

X. WHEEL OF FORTUNE

Nothing is lost, nothing is created, everything is transformed.

Antoine Lavoisier

Life cycles

Life gives us something, we lose it, we suffer, we learn to take care of things, we open up to somebody, we get hurt, we endure, we learn to forgive ourselves, we close up, we shut up, we open up, we learn to give. Nothing is written in stone. **This card's energy represents permanent impermanence: one day we win unexpectedly and are on top of the world; the next day we lose everything and we plunge to the depths.** We should accept change and not cling to nostalgia. This card calls for maturity. At the end of a cycle, it is important to reflect and ask who helped you get there; and if there were situations that slowed down your arrival, who opposed your progress?

The card

A wheel floats on moving waters. The three characters are trying to balance. The two on the sides adjusting their positions in order to stay standing, while the girl on top enjoys the view and her apparent stability. Who is in charge of the wheel?

Wheel of Fortune in a reading about love

Today you are looking for love; tomorrow is another day. With every sunrise, new forms of love are created. **Don't be frustrated when things change. Recycle your energy.** Remember not to be dragged down by a lack of love. You can take control.

Reversed meaning

An emotional conundrum. Being lost, turning in circles, not being able to see the bigger picture. **When you are stuck, this card speaks of repetitiveness**, leading you to choose your current discomfort rather than making the movements that are needed in order to change. I call this the "discomfort zone".

Advice

There is a bigger plan. Surrender to it. Interrupt the circular motion. **The wheel can represent an ascending spiral of personal growth as well as a vicious circle.** Love the process. There's no point in focusing only on results.

In a reading

The question that usually arises when this card appears in a reading is: when do you stop learning and start repeating yourself? Here are some other questions: what is making you uncomfortable? What changes do you refuse to acknowledge? When this card is the last one of your reading, my suggestion is to draw an extra card from the deck. The idea is not to be caught forever in the circular motion.

Astrological correspondence

This arcanum is associated with Jupiter. Expanding, trusting and directing are some of the key functions of this planet whose role is to make sense of all our actions. Jupiter finds faith in little things and hints at moving beyond the normal limits. It makes us special beings. The planet also has a promising motto: "Believing is creating."

A curious fact that helped me understand this card

>•>

In the OK Tarot deck, Adam J. Kurtz illustrates the tenth arcanum with a kind of compass-clock and the phrase "Time to move on". He reminds us that there is limited time on Earth, reinforcing the idea that our existence is temporary. In the Marseilles Tarot, this card shows **three creatures going up, down and standing on the wheel.** It reveals we are in constant movement and therefore should not take anything for granted. The creature going down on the left reminds us of being rooted and grounded. The one on the right refers to spiritualizing and trying to elevate ourselves. The creature on top has a sword the same size as The Magician's wand, but it also reminds us of the main element in Justice. What happened to the impressive arcanum and her sword (an emblem of subjectivity) two cards before? Now, the ego is reduced. The universe is too vast.

Living the energy of Wheel of Fortune

Write down everything you thought you would have achieved by this age when you were a kid. Make a detailed list. Analyze if any of those preconceptions still affect you today and if you need to say goodbye to some or even all of them. Is there anything you tell yourself you should do by a certain age that is making you uncomfortable? See which ideas limit you and which ones help you grow. Keep only the latter, cross out the rest and let go of them.

XI. STRENGTH

Strength does not come from physical capacity. It comes from an indomitable will.

Mahatma Gandhi

Wisdom

The dynamics of Tarot show that nothing is linear in this life. When we rest or stop to think, we are represented by arcana with even numbers, especially of the second and fourth degree, like The High Priestess, The Hanged Man, The Emperor and Temperance. But, after a time of calm, it's time to energize, to activate and become more proactive. That is Strength: **a new creative beginning, with more focus and, above all, with more courage.** This card invites us to target what we wish for, to confront and conquer it. The challenge is to master our passion and follow our instincts without letting the energy overflow.

The card

A magician wearing a hat in the shape of the infinity symbol uses her hands to open a lion's mouth while holding the animal down with her legs. Whether the beast is about to devour her or to surrender to her taming is yet to be seen.

Strength in a reading about love

Relax and enjoy. It is time to listen to your body. Surrender, don't judge yourself, don't be afraid to open up, don't be afraid of ridicule. Don't just text, organize a date. Or not. Make time for yourself: this is an opportunity to get to know yourself better.

Reversed meaning

Beware of harsh words. Don't say things that could hurt others. **Use your strength to build bridges, not to tear everything down.** Don't let your ego overwhelm you. Listen to your heart.

Advice

It's time to follow your instincts and your creativity. It is not time to calculate, think or hesitate. Surrender to the power of your energy and **obey the powerful will that encourages you to feel more alive.** In other words, face the music.

In a reading

Ask yourself which of the characters in this card represents you. Are you the lion that is refusing to obey or the brave tamer? What are you doing to conquer your dreams? Do you feel you are the author of your achievements or is life controlling you? **Is your head your ally or is it abandoning you?** It's time to behave creatively, think outside the box, take a risk. Your instinct knows best.

Astrological correspondence

This arcanum is associated with the energy of Leo, the second fire sign. What Strength and Leo have in common is self-confidence, the ability not to shrink in the face of life's challenges, to stand out with abundance and presence.

A curious fact that helped me understand this card

>•>•>•>•>•>•>>•>•>•>•>•>•>•>•>•>•>•>•>>•>•>•>•>•>•>•>>•>•>•>•>•>•>•>

For those who are critical of the dark magician Aleister Crowley, his illustration of Strength is more evidence of how he perverted Tarot, taking the vices of his own life to the design of the deck. In fact, in the Thoth deck, Strength is called Lust and shows a naked woman riding a lion. There is no moral judgement in his idea; it merely demonstrates the morals and the prejudice of those who despise his version of the card. At an exhibition of the cards, a child asked the illustrator about the naked woman riding the lion. She replied: How do you feel if you see some delicious-looking chocolates? You try them to see how good they taste. This is a picture of how you feel about those chocolates.

Living the energy of Strength

Play your favourite song and dance as if there was no tomorrow. Sing at the top of your voice. Dance to life's rhythms. Take a while to laugh about yourself and enjoy. Shake off all the drama.

THE HANGED MAN

XII. THE HANGED MAN

Let everything flow and nothing affect you.

Rest

When faced with this even-numbered card, it is time to make a stop. Sometimes we need to gather some more knowledge or pause to understand more about ourselves. **In order to adopt a new viewpoint, it is necessary to wait hanging upside down.** If you don't pause voluntarily, life will invite you to do so. The point is that there are probably big transformations coming and this is the calm you need before the storm.

The card

Although the man seems to be suspended from a thread, he is hanging comfortably. His legs are forming a number four, indicating stability. Even if others are worried about him or want to pull him down, The Hanged Man seems undisturbed by his position. With his hands tied and his ears uncovered, this means that it's time for listening rather than taking action. This position is also the only way of having your heart above your head. It is an invitation to make decisions with your heart. The wands on his side symbolize mother and father, with six open wounds on each side. What are the wounds on your family tree? It's time to understand where we come from.

The Hanged Man in a reading about love

You can look strange on the outside and be rich inside. This card invites you to accompany others in silence. If one of the two people seems unmotivated or withdrawn, they may be undergoing a personal process. **It is worth asking yourself what change is brought about by that apparently dead time.** Maybe one of you is making too many sacrifices just to keep things going.

Reversed meaning

Never-ending procrastination. **Unwillingness to act, a continuation of the resting that was initially attractive and necessary.** Laziness, emptiness and lack of motivation or attention end up making people around you want to act for you.

Advice

It is not time to choose or decide. **Sometimes it's necessary not to do anything.** Listen to yourself. Something is settling down. It's time to be a witness and not a protagonist.

In a reading

Pay attention to the card drawn after the twelfth arcanum. **It will make sense of the wait, or at least provide clues on how to analyze this pause.** Sometimes, the Tarot may indicate a loss of material wealth (hanging upside down, coins will drop from your pockets) or even anxiety as a result of so much passivity.

Astrological correspondence

This arcanum is associated with water, the element of the signs of Cancer, Scorpio and Pisces. Water represents the emotional world, both the flow of emotions and emotions that are stuck. This element adopts the shape of its container. On the one hand, this reflects water's ability to adapt. On the other hand, it hints at quietness. Water also has a kind of gift for softening harsh textures.

A curious fact that helped me understand this card

>•>•>•>•>•>>•>•>•>•>•>>•>•>•>•>•>>•>•>•>•>•>>•>•>•>•>•>>•>

I once came across an artist's Tarot in which Jackson Pollock was The Hanged Man. The reason for this choice is that throughout his life he worked on his creations without following the rules. He laid his canvas on the floor and began dripping paint in a kind of primitive dance, both original and genuine. Pollock can be compared to The Hanged Man because he worked in his world and the rest happened "as if by magic". If you get this card, you can ask yourself the following: can you develop your own point of view on things? Take a break until you discover the answer.

Living the energy of The Hanged Man

Do you remember when we were little and technology was not around us all the time? We got bored. And boredom triggered creative activities: jumping so as not to step on lines, counting signs on the street, even building houses. Let's practise creative leisure. Spend a day not doing anything. Get bored and let what happens surprise you.

XIII

DEATH

XIII. DEATH

Be the change you wish to see in the world.

Transformation

The philosopher Martin Heidegger said we are "being toward death". Wherever we are on life's journey, death remains inevitable. Our desire to avoid it pushes us toward honesty. In *Jung and Tarot*, Nichols analyzes the poem "Death" by W. B. Yeats, and notes that death, as a unique event inevitably happening at a certain point in time, is a human concept and therefore we should not fear it. She concludes by saying that death is in fact a continual process, intertwined with life and, as Yeats says, we can die many times. **In fact, everything we know experiences micro-deaths, as it mutates and stops being as we know it.** For many people, this card is "the arcanum with no name", but I think we should call its name. Why should we assume that living with no risk is worse than dying?

The card

A skeleton moves forward with its scythe, in a similar pose to The Fool, forced to step on the fragments of a life it is leaving behind. The scythe symbolizes the deep cleansing this arcanum brings about. We can no longer keep brushing the things that bother us under the carpet. There are little flowers on the path, ready to re-sprout from the ashes. Also, two heads rise up from the ground: they are a man and a woman, symbolizing the authority figures we have had to confront.

Death in a reading about love

This card speaks of intensity and drama. If there is an encounter, it will be visceral. The touch of flesh, pain, base instincts, human misery. If there is disagreement, you are being asked to challenge the way things are: **allow yourself to plunge into a crisis.**

Reversed meaning

Like a birth that does not want to be natural, in reverse, this card means pent-up energy that cannot find a way to escape. It explodes in anger, it rots. **In a stuck position, this card speaks of not wanting to accept change.** Trying to cover up something that is bad will only prolong the torment.

Advice

Leave your fear behind. Be ready to accept the change that is coming. **You need to let go of the inertia left by The Hanged Man and let something die in order for something new to be born.** The process hurts, but it will make you grow. It is a strong and clear calling to cherish each new day.

In a reading

A revolution is necessary to bring inner cleansing. It's time to wake up, to lift up that carpet under which you hid everything you didn't understand. Symbolically, it's the end of childhood. It's important to pay attention to other cards in order to see what needs to be discarded, freed or kept.

Astrological correspondence

Scorpio, the second water sign, knows how to find its way in the dark depths of the soul. Its relentless will can face any pain and give in to moments of intensity. Scorpio has a great capacity to change and be reborn.

A curious fact that helped me understand this card

>•>

Silke is a textile artist born in Austria, who has lived and developed all her work in Argentina. Her work arises from a relationship with the spiritual world that has enabled her to channel her own version of the major arcana in the form of 22 huge silk tapestries. In her deck, Death is white and transmits light. Remarkably, there is no scythe on this card. Instead, there is a resting body, apparently undergoing a meditative reset. Only an arm is skeletal. Her head and torso retain the silhouette of a human body. This reinforces the idea that this arcanum invites us to repair and improve. If we don't open up to this awareness, we may gradually die.

Living the energy of Death

Think about your biggest fear today. Take a sheet of paper and draw it, name it and briefly describe it. How does it make you feel? Think of ways of fighting it. When you are ready, let go of it. Tear the drawing into pieces and say goodbye.

XIV. TEMPERANCE

Tenderness is the opposite of taking position; it means accepting what is there and being touched by it.

Cecilia Pavón

Emotional stability

The transformation proposed by Death has left its scars and this great Tarot angel will help us heal. To grow stronger is to understand that the two ends touch; there is no break if we accept the whole. In order to heal, we need to be willing to compromise. Nobody is right; the value lies in sharing. We should not mistake this energy for signs of frailty. It takes a lot of courage to lick your own wounds. Just as The Emperor (fourth arcanum) speaks of stability in the material sphere; ten steps later, Temperance says: *in medio stat virtus:* the best option is in the middle ground.

The card

A woman with a peaceful expression pours water from one pot to another, enriching both. The protagonist of this card is water, the main source of life. As the fourteenth card, Temperance includes the number four: stability in the emotional sphere.

Temperance in a reading about love

Do you feel you are in good hands? **This card tells you somebody wants to take care of you.** Give in to their embrace. Don't let fear cool things down.

Reversed meaning

Living in the clouds, looking down on everyone, **not being aware of complaints or your own wishes; these are examples of the reverse meaning of this card.** Too much water can be overwhelming, and it can disconnect you from your personal passions.

Advice

Find harmony. Balance your energy. Respond to the call for calm. **Be patient and trusting. Somewhere somebody is protecting you.** It's time to let it flow.

In a reading

This is a call to bring opposites together: reconciliation, negotiation, healing. On the one hand, the card calls for self-control. On the other, it foretells good outcomes. It invites you to connect with tenderness and have gentle thoughts.

Astrological correspondence

Temperance is associated with Sagittarius, the third fire sign. It is a contained fire, harmonious and controlled. This zodiac sign has traits of wisdom, optimism and expansion. In Sagittarius, everything seems to be solved favourably for all parts.

A curious fact that helped me understand this card

>·>

Aleister Crowley, creator of Thoth Tarot, called this card Art, rather than Temperance (as it's called in some decks), which gives a sense of ubiquity, or The Temperance, as the personification of calm in a particular subject. Crowley's reason for this has to do with connecting the fourteenth arcanum to his definition of magic ("magick"): the art and science of making change happen according to your will. Alchemists defined their role as the art of combining elements. The two hardest to integrate were water and fire, the elements that the fourteenth arcanum mysteriously speak to. In the card, water is in plain sight. It's what's circulating between the pots. But what about fire? When this card appears in a reading, I like to ask: where is your fire?

Living the energy of Temperance

Build your own altar. Find a quiet place in your house. Add an inspiring picture, something you would like to honour or need to remember. Choose objects representing each element: earth can be a plant, petals or a stone. Water could be a nice perfume in oil. Fire is added by a candle. Air is brought by incense. Write down an intention, something you want to heal or you need to focus on. Every day, take a moment to light the candle and connect to your intention. You can leave your Tarot deck there, feeding on all that concentrated creative energy.

THE DEVIL

XV. THE DEVIL

The only way to get rid of a temptation is to yield to it.

Oscar Wilde

. . . .

Seduction games

Morality, the mind, desire and power intertwine in this arcanum, creating a maze of tension. **Usually, this is sexual tension. What would we be without ambition, pleasure or fantasy?** Here, morality is defeated and what is forbidden prevails. If Temperance is light, it is only because there's a dark side. In fact, if the fourteenth arcanum wonders where the inner fire is in the face of so much restraint, wise Tarot replies: "Here". The Devil sets in motion an engine that awakens passion. Will you censor it? Remember that sexual energy is also creative energy, an invitation to explore everything we feel curious about. The question posed by this card is: how far are we willing to go to get what we crave? This arcanum blurs the boundaries between good and bad. As Oscar Wilde would say: "Every saint has a past, and every sinner has a future."

The card

The Devil is the counterpart of the fifth arcanum, The Hierophant. Half-human, half-creature, this eight-eyed figure is vigilant. Apart from the ones on her face, The Devil has an eye on each breast, two eyes on her belly and one on each knee. With so many eyes, her prey is unlikely to escape. She seems to be tying two people together. What we don't yet know is if they are able to untie themselves. Are they imprisoned or is it a game?

The Devil in a reading about love

Passion, sex, seduction, possession, body, desire. Intelligent and arrogant, this Devil does not give in to anybody. **In a reading, this card represents a challenge to preconceptions: how much fun you are having and how much of it is vice.** Is it magnetism or deceit? It may be your chance to redefine the terms of the relationship.

Reversed meaning

You may be projecting your own weaknesses, **believing that evil is only on the outside when it also lies within your own beliefs.** The card may indicate vice, addiction, fraud, abuse, betrayal, dependence, gluttony and excesses in general. Self-punishment and censorship are not the solution. Allow yourself to have fun. **Be free: chains are bonds that only exist in your head.** Empower yourself. You can be in control.

In a reading

What is your role in this triangle of tension? This divine trio is here to show you something. First, you are warned not to submit to another person's power. Then, you are invited to make use of your talent. Respond to a challenge in business, a call for creativity and the joy of your vocation.

Astrological correspondence

This arcanum is associated with Capricorn, the last earth sign in the zodiac wheel, making use of your resources in order to reach the top. An old joke says a Capricorn's marital status is neither single nor married, but "building an empire". This is the same way in which The Devil sees leadership.

A curious fact that helped me understand this card

>•>

Only a few decks have applied substantial changes to the fifteenth arcanum. I once saw an image online of a Tarot deck made up of cats, where The Devil was a golden retriever. I found the contrast funny: what for many humans is the most adorable dog can be the worst nuisance for a different species. This opens up a philosophical debate: is there such a thing as absolute good or evil, or is villainy relative? If evil is relative, is there a boundary that cannot be crossed? In any case, the design of *Enchantress Tarot* attempts to question fixed ideas about what is evil. Like the next step after The Empress, The Devil calls for personal empowerment first.

Living the energy of The Devil

How long has it been since you learned something new? What is stopping you? It may be learning a new language, eating something new, texting a person you like but you don't dare approach. What would you do if you weren't afraid? Today, take a new look at your wardrobe. Match your clothes in a more daring way and go out on the street feeling like a warrior. You can do it. Don't be afraid.

THE TOWER

XVI. THE TOWER

God is dead.

Friedrich Nietzsche

. . . .

Drama

Something that was tightly sealed breaks apart. An ancient structure cracks, revealing its secrets. Energy is released. The Devil has been playing in the dark and The Tower can no longer hold everything inside. **A search for new, deeper foundations has started.** When Nietzsche said: "God is dead", he was referring to the values of the nineteenth century. Societies based on divine order were coming to an end. It was time to start thinking about a scale of individual values. This card presents you with the question of what you will believe in after your personal apocalypse. Everything becomes a battlefield. It's not punishment, but an invitation to find yourself again.

The card

A medieval tower has just a few windows at the top. Two people are falling from it, headfirst. Did they fall because they were tormented? Did somebody push them? What were they escaping? Their hands reach the ground first, allowing them to take root. If we scan the card from top to bottom, we will see these people's hearts are above their heads. The roof of the tower has fallen; it's time for a change.

The Tower in a reading about love

If the question is about a stable couple, it seems it is time to look again at the basis and the conditions of this contract before Troy burns. If the reading is about somebody new, pay attention: **this person may be entering your life in order to break apart something that was deeply embedded in your life, or they may put up barriers.**

Reversed meaning

Not knowing how to handle change. **Secretly insisting on the safety of The Tower.** In reverse, this card warns about holding on to something that is false, experiencing everything as a great loss and not thinking about the opportunity to reinvent yourself. As on the negative side of Wheel of Fortune, inhabiting the "discomfort zone".

Advice

A change is coming. **It's time to unmask a truth,** to be brave, show yourself and break free. There's no point staying in your safe tower, looking out of the window. If you don't take action, the attack will come from outside.

In a reading

If we take The Tower as a symbol of our body, this card may be warning about somatization – experiencing psychological distress as physical symptoms. **If The Tower is the first card of the reading, it means you have a winding path ahead. If it is the last one, it means rigid structures will fall.** If you can receive this card in its luminous aspect and are willing to accept the challenge it represents, you'll experience the energy of The Tower as a party. If, for some reason, you feel that what is happening is too big a change and you resist it, you will face a considerable crisis. But, as the feminist movement says of patriarchy: it will fall.

Astrological correspondence

Mars is the planet of action, desire and conquest. It shows us our attitude in battle, the force that drives us toward life. It means using our physicality and marking the territory occupied by our body, our energy and our intentions. The red planet asks us: what is your leadership style?

A curious fact that helped me understand this card

>•>

In some Egyptian decks, the sixteenth arcanum is called Frailty and its image is an obelisk with a crack on top, as if it were an Eastern vase about to break due to the impact of a bolt of lightning. There is an astrological reference that claims a connection between Mercury and The Tower. This refers to the fact that the world is a mental construction. The image of the obelisk allows me to see that each brick in The Tower is an additional block in our construction of meaning and, from time to time, we are invited to jump out of it and lose control. When we do, what falls is not the building of "truth", but the concept that we had of such a building.

Living the energy of The Tower

Picture your best self: what changes would you need to make in order to become that person? Which people would no longer be around you? Write down a few words to free yourself from everything you are holding on to that is doing you harm. What could change to give you a more authentic life that is full of purpose? Choose a title for the structures that need to fall and, in an act of psycho-magic, burn the piece of paper on which you wrote everything down.

XVII. THE STAR

What you give, you give to yourself.

Alejandro Jodorowsky

. . . .

Authenticity

Bring yourself into the world. Find your gift. **The Star means finding who you came here to be.** In this card, there is a synchronicity with the universe, which seems to blink a cosmic eye and say, "You are where you are supposed to be." After the explosion and fall of The Tower, your environment invites you to inhabit a calm and prosperous space. In such an environment, you are ready to share your gifts. In The Chariot, you search for monetary exchange or concrete acknowledgement of your achievements. In The Star, you do things without asking for anything in return. Giving becomes something genuine, like a natural consequence of your being. This energy nourishes and purifies. Your internal Shaman, fertile, authentic and free, makes you accept that vulnerability is a source of power. With this card, you love what you do and do what you love, and, without bragging, are acknowledged for that.

The card

Ten cards on, we meet a seven again, a symbol of victory, this time in the celestial sphere. The protagonist is a naked woman. Her enlarged navel is a symbol of fertility. She is holding two pots, from which water is flowing, just as her essence merges with the flow of life. A large star and seven sister stars guide her in the sky. The little bird on the card represents freedom and also reminds you that you had to go through the crisis in the thirteenth arcanum in order to find your identity.

The Star in a reading about love

Welcome to romance with no reservations. Everything suggests you will be able to show yourself and comfortably express everything that once made you self-conscious. **Natural and intuitive, this relationship may give new**

meaning to your world. If there is nothing new in love, you should pay attention to the nostalgic aspect of The Star: the woman may be pouring water into the rivers of the past.

Reversed meaning

A girl of a thousand wounds. When stuck, this energy implies over-giving, always running after love, wasting the energy and resources around us. In reverse, this card warns about idealizing people, seeing them as shining and being **unable to see your own brilliance.**

Advice

Acknowledge your beauty. **The constellations in the universe come together in your favour.** You no longer need to ask for permission to shine.

In a reading

There is the opportunity to create something new. **The question is: what will you give birth to? Creativity, a pregnancy, connecting with nature and the beautiful aspects of yourself are possible answers.** The card also suggests hope, opening up to reconciliation. If you are feeling nostalgic, ask yourself how to take advantage of what you have, rather than longing for what you have lost.

Astrological correspondence

This arcanum is associated with Aquarius, the last air sign, and characterized by its collective energy and awareness of the contribution of an individual to a group. Aquarius people are often interested in the well-being of everyone or inhabiting utopian worlds. Many times, they are eccentric, with a generous spirit, just like the girl in The Star.

A curious fact that helped me understand this card

>⦁>⦁>⦁>⦁>⦁>>⦁>⦁>>⦁>⦁>>⦁>⦁>>⦁>⦁>>⦁>⦁>>⦁>⦁>>⦁>⦁>⦁>⦁>⦁>⦁>⦁>⦁>>⦁>

When studying the minor arcana, I discovered some features of the suits and of some cards in particular that enabled me to see the major arcana with new eyes. For example, Ace of Cups changed the way I saw The Star. The flowing water in that card may represent the waste or bad management of resources sometimes evidenced by the seventeenth arcanum. Seeing both cards in the context of the scarcity of water in the world may bring anguish. However, Israel's treatment of water is like The Star in its splendour and hope; it is a guiding light. In 2023, 85 per cent of water entering homes in Israel came from the sea, after a desalination treatment deemed impossible by science just a few years ago.

Living the energy of The Star

Be brave and try an alternative therapy that interests you, something that connects you to your light, your purpose. In order to balance the heart, mind and body, I recommend floral therapy or a good reading of the Akashic records to open up to the mysteries of the soul. To give love to your vital energy and for guaranteed relaxation, you could try a reiki session.

THE MOON

XVIII. THE MOON

How will you go about finding that thing the nature of which is totally unknown to you?

Meno

Sensitive world

You go to bed with something in mind. You take a deep breath, visualize it, mumble something and your eyelids fall. Suddenly, you fall too, just as Alice fell down the rabbit hole. **When you wake up, you are huge, or tiny. Or are you still dreaming? Or do you wake up, go about your routine and, at the end of the day, wonder if all that was somebody else's dream?** This mental chaos is The Moon: mystery, fantasy, the art of philosophizing aimlessly, what you reflect and attract, magnetism, surrealism and what we subconsciously struggle to hide. However, you can value what is hidden as a challenge on the road, a test for the explorer in you. In her book *A Field Guide to Getting Lost,* Rebecca Solnit speaks about what we lose and about losing ourselves. Quoting Meno, she also wonders how we go about searching for something whose nature is unknown to us. Moving through darkness, with no guarantees, is a necessary part of every journey.

The card

The sixteenth arcanum had one tower. The Moon has two: one is open to the skies, the other is closed. There is a winding path of water, two dogs (or wolves, in some decks) and a scorpion in the middle. On that winding path, everything seems to symbolize imminent danger. The towers are there, but they offer only deceptive shelter. Do we want to inhabit those rigid structures again, the ones we struggled to leave behind just two cards ago? This card is an invitation to become intuitive in the darkness. The dogs can't be tricked; they would know us in any disguise.

The Moon in a reading about love

Is the person you've just seen hyper-magnetic or has your mind fallen for fascination again? **The connection may be sensual or completely confusing.** Think about whether maternal feelings are your thing or how long you can accept such a changeable dynamic? As Lord Henry said to Dorian Gray in the iconic novel by Oscar Wilde: "You will always be fond of me. I represent to you all the sins you never had the courage to commit."

Reversed meaning

Madness, disorientation, anguish, addiction, hidden fear and overflowing emotions. In reverse, this card tells you it is important to look into your nightmares. **When we get lost in a search within ourselves, the result is either depression or despair.**

Advice

If what you see is not helping, **connect to what you can't see.** Openness and intuition. Once you bring together the aspects of yourself, you will find the peace of mind you've longed for.

In a reading

What is asking to come to light and what remains hidden? **Art, poetry, music, inexplicable attraction, subtlety, dark sciences, children.** The Moon asks you to consider your connection to these sensitive topics. When we talk about darkness, we think about disguise, elements we have rejected, fears and the indecipherable mental labyrinth.

Astrological correspondence

Pisces is the last sign in the zodiac wheel and it belongs to the element of water. As such, it refers to the world of emotions, intuition and sensitivity. The energetic frequency of Pisces is so loving that, often, Pisces people are too empathetic and may then suffer as they absorb other people's suffering. However, well channelled and illuminated by the Moon, Pisces' creative and spiritual potential is huge.

A curious fact that helped me understand this card

>•>

In her book *Jung and Tarot*, Nichols says, as if she were speaking for The Moon: "Why would Man aspire to conquer superior regions, when He has not solved his ecology problems on Earth?" This reminds me that, after piloting the aircraft to the Moon in 1969, Michael Collins said that, from above, the Earth looked fragile. Buzz Aldrin, the second man to step on the Moon after Neil Armstrong, suffered a breakdown and severe depression as a consequence of leaving the planet. The Moon arcanum warns you that getting close to the unknown requires plenty of emotional and spiritual support.

Living the energy of The Moon

Do you dare to find beauty in subtlety? For a whole day, pay attention to the things you see on the street, the books you come across, the leaves that have fallen from the trees and how the rays of the sun change as the hours pass. Everything is part of your path. During the night, when everything is turned off, observe the dim lights that are still shining. At the next full Moon, take advantage of the ultimate of subtleties and look for a quiet place outdoors to contemplate the Moon. What message does it give to you?

XIX

THE SUN

XIX. THE SUN

It is strength to laugh and to abandon oneself, to be light.

Frida Kahlo

. . . .

Being

We take for granted waking up every day. Taking a step, moving in a certain direction, realizing our projects: none of these just happen, just because you are alive. They are voluntary acts that require energy. Enthusiasm, joy and renewal are just around the corner if you know how to find them. **The energy of The Sun proposes unconditional self-love, the chance to reset with every sunrise.** Once you have reached The Sun, you have left behind the complex depth of The Moon, and this arcanum invites you to share with others, to play, to demonstrate everything you have learned along the way, without prejudice, restraint or delusions of grandeur.

The card

The protagonists of this card are two naked children. They look like twins helping each other. They may represent a couple, a pair of colleagues or two friends. The Sun illuminates the scene and looks you in the face. A question arises about the symmetry of the relationship. Does the Sun rise for all of us in the same way?

The Sun in a reading about love

Both characters in this card seem to shine with their own light. They are transparent, graceful and honest. **The Sun is an invitation to be genuine and generous with our peers.** The challenge is not to hold an idealized picture of them, not to become a fatherly figure or to fall into the asymmetrical dynamics of master and follower.

Reversed meaning

Vanity and total self-obsession. **A stuck Sun represents an authoritarian or self-centred person who looks for applause and does not let others be**

themselves. Remember that, when something is illuminated, it naturally projects a shadow behind it. The Sun invites you to reflect on how you handle light. Are you always empathetic when somebody is overshadowed by your success?

Advice

You are already in a central position. Now it's time to learn to relate to others. **Or rather, accept the challenge of expressing a new version of yourself.** If you are a leader, allow others to lead you or vice versa. It is time to bring together these complementary energies.

In a reading

The Sun means solutions and companionship. Something will be achieved. **Success illuminates everything. There's a renewed feeling of winning and freedom.** As for companionship, you should learn how to value others. Even when you do things on your own, remember that you would be nothing without the company, validation or even rejection of others.

Astrological correspondence

In astrology, the sun shows us when we are the centre of our universe. Its light illuminates our purpose and encourages us to behave in authentic ways. That is the path to success. Applause is not earned by external features, as in The Chariot, but as a natural result of the light we give off by being ourselves.

A curious fact that helped me understand this card

In the Marseilles deck, The Sun is represented by two naked children, maybe a pair of twins, playing and sharing. As it turns out, the children have direct references to The Devil. One of the children has a devil tail, and both have marks on their necks, as those left by the cord the devil uses to hold the characters on the card. Alejandro Jodorowsky said of this card: "We may say that the energy held in the shadows in the fifteenth arcanum is now in broad daylight and, instead of a passionate subconscious relationship, these two

characters are based on mutual help and human love at its purest."
As in the connection between Death and The Star, we can see that in
order to shine, we need first to go through the dark journeys of life.

Living the energy of The Sun

Think of the virtues of people around you that you could imitate. What good
deed could you perform today? There may be somebody in need of a kind
gesture. Share a smile, give up your seat, talk to someone, give someone a
hug. Give away the best of yourself to the world and prepare to receive it back.

JUDGEMENT

XX. JUDGEMENT

Living is like tearing through a museum. Not until later do you really start absorbing what you saw.

Audrey Hepburn

. . . .

Understanding

Do you know what brought you here? What series of events made me write these words, have someone translate them and publish them for someone on the other side of the world with a book in their hands? What pushed us into the world of Tarot? Why haven't we come out of it yet? Judgement is a card that confronts us with all these questions and invites us to align who we are with what we think and do. It's a card that asks you to look at yourself carefully and embrace all aspects of yourself. You can only find your true vocation by understanding yourself. **Forgiving and accepting are necessary stages before you can taste the beginning of the end.** Or the beginning of the beginning. According to Alejandro Jodorowsky, every being that is born is wanted by divinity. That is what this card should make us feel with its divine calling. It is as if the universe could interact on social media and sent the message: "The universe likes your picture."

The card

A woman, a man and a little androgynous creature are naked, and facing the sky. Are they asking for redemption or receiving glory? The little creature in the card, with its back to us, represents the fruit of your personal project. An angel seems to make sense of everything with music that speaks directly to the soul. It is time for coming together and listening to the divine calling.

Judgement in a reading about love

Opportunities may occur for reunion and forgiveness, and answering the call of true love. **Fortunately, Tarot does not know whether you will find love with this person or someone new. You should take a leap of faith and open up to love.**

Reversed meaning

Not listening to the call, pretending that nothing has happened and expecting others to make a move are all pretty obvious ways of delaying the outcome. **Not accepting facts as they are, not coming to terms with things,** going through certain stages in life as if they are a formality are all examples of the reverse meaning of Judgement.

Advice

Give yourself permission to be. Be honest. **Look back at the path travelled and all its players. Don't avoid reality.** Forgive yourself. Leave guilt behind and confront everything. When we renew the wish to live, we can create something new.

In a reading

Listen to the calling. Look success in the face. This is the sound advice of Judgement. The card asks you to acknowledge this climatic moment. **If something is about to happen or come to an end, be prepared to do whatever it takes.** Pay attention to the signs, connect to the energy of celebration, be merciful (this is not the time to judge or be judged), work toward the common good. You will need plenty of awareness to experience what comes next in the deck: The World.

Astrological correspondence

Judgement is traditionally associated with fire. This element is the vital flame, capable of reducing everything to ashes or creating the spark of life. It burns according to the movement of the things around it; it has the power to illuminate and gather all of us around it. A more modern reading would be to associate Judgement to Chiron, the wounded healer. This planet invites us to reflect on the idea that we never heal individually. Our vulnerability is a magnet to attract other people, with whom we become strong.

A curious fact that helped me understand this card

>•>•>•>•>•>>•>•>•>•>•>>•>•>•>•>•>>•>•>•>•>•>>•>•>•>•>•>>•>

OK Tarot has the most minimalist illustrations I've ever seen in a deck. Kurtz uses just two colours: a pink background and black line drawings. In this deck, the twentieth arcanum is an old hand mirror. As soon as I saw this image I thought of the classic quote: "Mirror, mirror, on the wall, who's the fairest of them all?" Judgement is an invitation to look at ourselves in the mirror, to make a kind but serious examination of ourselves and, above all, to accept the image the mirror shows us – whatever it may be.

Living the energy of Judgement

Write a "sorry letter" to yourself: make a list of all those things you think you've done wrong or you could have done better. Then forgive yourself. Treat yourself with love and compassion. Read the letter out loud in front of the mirror as many times as you need to.

XXI

THE WORLD

XXI. THE WORLD

Independence is happiness.

Susan B. Anthony

. . . .

Vital orgasm

According to the humanist psychologist Abraham Maslow, self-actualization – the realization of our potential – is among the higher order of our needs. After eating, living in a safe home, being part of a community with a sense of belonging, and material success, we are confronted with the idea of actualization. The World proposes that **creativity, spontaneity, open-mindedness and freedom are the ways to broaden our horizons after achieving our more basic goals.** We should enjoy this brief victory because it is the end of a long journey and, just like an orgasm, it fades away in a breath. The feeling of glory present in the twenty-first arcanum could also be seen as an achievement in the fight for equality (such as the achievements of Susan B. Anthony).

The card

A naked woman swims inside an oval made of laurel. Is the oval an expanded version of The High Priestess' egg? The woman is holding a stick in one hand, a symbol of her capacity for action, and a cup in the other one, a symbol of receptivity. Four figures protect the woman. They represent the four elements: the lion stands for fire, the eagle for air, the angel is water and the bull is earth.

The World in a reading about love

Feeling fulfilled may bring new opportunities in love. When faced with this card, some people talk about marriage. I would say union is possible as long as you are able to share your fulfilment. This card offers a home: would you open the doors to another person?

Reversed meaning

The oval in the card may represent a comfort zone. **Staying still and warm is a way of avoiding all kinds of growth.** With this attitude, your perception of the world will always be the same. That is understandable. After all, who wants to move away from success and glory? Tarot is wise and will soon send you the archetype of The Fool to push you into an uncertain adventure.

Advice

Surrender. You have everything you need in order to do so. **In Judgement, you had understanding. Now it's time to experience *joie de vivre*.** They say the world is at your feet. If you cannot see that yet, are you capable of going to check it out?

In a reading

The time is right for unity, a journey, a birth, an orgasm. When this is the first card of the reading, it means something needs to be closed before what's coming can see the light. It's a sign that the new cycle is taking its time. **Maybe you still have something to give where you are.** When The World is the last card of the reading, it means expression and synthesis, dedication and alignment. The card calls you to accept the challenge of total love. You are ready for it.

Astrological correspondence

This arcanum is associated with Saturn. It may seem strange to associate the planet of maturity and structure as the principal of this arcanum that expresses so much pleasure. However, do remember that boundaries are needed before we are able to create and that discipline helps us to carry out our projects. Saturn is often associated with earthly matters thanks to its ability to make you confront reality and not get lost in fantasy. The World could also be associated with the Earth, as in the egg we inhabit.

A curious fact that helped me understand this card

In the Artists Tarot by Fera (a deck combining visual artists with the arcana), Vincent van Gogh is The World, surrounded by the four elements. Fire led his artistic drive – he painted frenetically all day long. Air made him come and go between sanity and insanity – he was admitted to a psychiatric institution for months. Water was present in the sensitivity of his every stroke. But it was only after death that the energy of earth arrived. That's when he was acknowledged, and his works were sold for vast sums of money. In order to experience the glory of the twenty-second arcanum, it's not enough to find our talent and offer it to the world, as happens in The Star. We need to do the creative and physical work, continue to do so through time, surround ourselves with the right people and ask for the necessary help to reach the top.

Living the energy of The World

Take The World and The Fool. Shuffle them and see the order in which they appear. If The World appears first, something is finishing and it's time to take a step forward, to accept the adventure of doing something new. Take your time, as The Fool does. If The World is the second card, it's a moment of fulfilment. It's time to rest and enjoy your gifts.

MINOR ARCANA

The minor arcana are numbered from one to ten. As in the original Spanish deck, there are four suits: wands, swords, cups and pentacles. **Each number within the suit can be expressed by a verb, and each suit is the energy that influences the action. These combinations create 40 scenarios of everyday life.** For example, aces "enable" and the wand suit channels desire. Therefore, Ace of Wands may mean **being able to wish.** In a reading, we use the minor arcana to get details about the major arcana. Like houses in astrology, the minor arcana is the area in which energy unfolds.

The last major arcanum, The World, left us both elated and confined. We need the eagerness and the vital drive of wands to restart the energy flow.

Wands

Let's start with wands. Without desire, there is nothing. This suit represents **fire, enthusiasm, drive and strength.** There is no logical explanation as to what makes us move; it is like a primary instinct, we simply feel it. It's like spring.

Swords

This suit represents **intellect, and the strategy and ideas that we develop after a little reasoning.** Everything is in the air: our mind is where our rational decisions arise from, but is also the source of anguish and mental suffering. Just as illnesses come in winter.

Cups

At the end of all our thoughts, we realize we need to feel. This suit does not represent a brief impulse as in wands, but something deeper: **feeling touched, flowing, being affected by others.** Water running and clearing the way, as in autumn.

Pentacles

Finally, we come into contact with what can be seen, touched or managed. This suit represents **earth, body, home, money, time and routine.** We spread out all our resources in the earthly sphere. This suit is associated with the freshness of summer.

Note: there is no set order of the suits. This is just the order I suggest, in which energy starts to flow from desire and culminates in things being achieved. This is just a theory; in practice, it can work the other way round. For example, we may start with an idea (swords) and end up in wands, finding our desire.

ACE OF WANDS

Creative power: The card shows a hand grabbing a flowering wand. The palm is visible, which could be read as a sign of frankness. Your inner fire lights up: you desperately wish for something; you want it all. This card usually represents the subconscious impulse. Ace of Wands means great enthusiasm for the new. It suggests adventure, vitality and willingness.

Reversed meaning: You are incapable of taking action. Irrationality, inability to understand others, imposing your will on others.

Reading: Something is about to bloom. All this inner desire needs a safe channel in order to become real.

ACE OF WANDS

ACE OF SWORDS

ACE OF SWORDS

Mental clarity: On this card, the hand holding the sword comes from the past and we can see the back of the hand, which symbolizes the protection of ideas. You are assertive. Ideas, strategies, conquests: everything on the mental plane and relating to the use of words is flowing freely. You know what you want and you hold on to it firmly. The feeling is that of The Magician.

Reversed meaning: Coldness, verbal aggression, underestimating the intellect or adopting an extreme ideological stance.

Reading: This card is an invitation to put your ideas on the table.

ACE OF CUPS

Emotional abundance: An open hand holds a cup by its base as a symbol of surrender. In response, the water cascades down to nurture the surroundings, asking for nothing in return. This speaks of satisfaction, wholeness and love. Self-esteem and emotional experiences are among the topics of this card.

Reversed meaning: Getting lost in your inner labyrinth. Being hypersensitive or too changeable.

Reading: Devotion. Think about all the love you have and give. Do you feel comfortable with that or is it too much? Review the energy that you are absorbing from your surroundings.

ACE OF CUPS

ACE OF PENTACLES

Maximum capacity to achieve: The hand holds the pentacle as a symbol of possession. Remember that what you "have" includes both material things and also your body, time and life itself. You have prosperity, your goals have materialized. What you have is real; it's no longer a desire, an idea or a fantasy as in the previous aces. Your gaze rests on your resources and achievements.

Reversed meaning: Being wasteful is an obvious manifestation of a stuck Ace of Pentacles. It may also mean lack of achievement, lack of connection between the spiritual world and what you possess, or bad use of your time.

Reading: Material abundance in a project, love, work, family or anything else you have set your mind on.

ACE OF PENTACLES

Aces represent the potential to create. They bring the virtues of desire, ideas, emotion and the possibility of realizing projects.

TWO OF WANDS

Mastery: This card suggests the appearance of another person in a new field of experience. Will you partner up or finally ask for the help you need? The energy of this card means focusing on what you want from the safety of home. In that comfortable place, everything seems possible. We are complex beings made of coexisting complementary forces.

Reversed meaning: Feeling you have to choose for somebody else, feeling the burden of another person. In its negative aspect, this card may also represent rivalry. It requires work on your inner self.

Reading: Audacity and vision. Will you embrace the adventure? Don't forget to use all the versions of yourself.

TWO OF WANDS

TWO OF SWORDS

Mental void: The card shows a woman resting with her eyes closed. Above her head we can see two crossed swords. On the one hand, she cannot act; on the other hand, she wants to. This block is, however, at least for now, only in the mind. Often, we choose to avoid our emotions in order to avoid conflict. This is the scattering or hiding of feelings. It's hard to tell if this is peace or emptiness, as could be experienced in The Hanged Man.

Reversed meaning: Fantasy. There are emotions hidden behind all this logic.

Reading: This is not the time to make decisions. It's a time for ambiguity, knowing that no one can be sure of the outcome.

TWO OF SWORDS

TWO OF CUPS

Daydream: Two young women join together in a spiritual ceremony. Each of them is holding her cup as a sign of sharing their most precious treasure: their emotions. This card represents a moment of closeness, intimacy and connection.

Reversed meaning: You don't know how to handle your emotions. In its negative aspect, this card represents Oedipal love, projecting a familiar structure on a new person you've met, or becoming possessive.

Reading: Longing. If there's a union, it's blessed. You have your family's support. It's a moment when protection is valuable. What are you hiding away?

TWO OF CUPS

TWO OF PENTACLES

Juggler: A girl juggles with two gold coins. Does this harlequin entertain us or excite us? Does she make us feel stressed or is she reflecting something of ourselves? We survive by trying to balance everything that is important in our lives. This card represents the typical moment of wondering: what shall I do with all this? Something wants to start growing. But, before it does so, we wonder what will happen.

Reversed meaning: You feel you need somebody else in order to leave the current situation behind. You are delayed because you are more interested in playing and experimenting than taking responsibility for those pentacles. Don't procrastinate.

Reading: You hesitate between what you want and what you have to do. You wonder who will compensate you for everything you are trying to do. Keep going. It's the only way of finding out.

TWO OF PENTACLES

Number two is receptive, always ready to open up to somebody else. It signifies inclusion and accumulation.

THREE OF WANDS

Drive: A young woman looks at a stimulating landscape, a field of possibilities. She is surrounded by three wands in bloom. You know those moments when you are just dying to try new things? That's the three of wands. Virtue, pleasure, group energy. Something starts to grow and calls you to join in. The feelings are similar to those represented by The Empress.

Reversed meaning: Being too pushy won't let you see other points of view. In its negative aspect, this card means excess. Three is a crowd.

Reading: It's time for stimulation and making a start. Accept the challenge and feel empowered. Become a leader of your group or the protagonist of something. This is a beginning of something that will do you good.

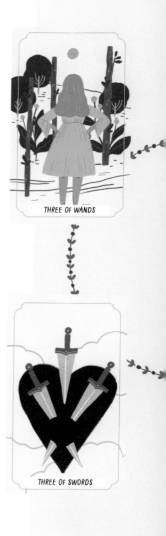

THREE OF WANDS

THREE OF SWORDS

Sorrow: Three swords penetrate a heart, so there is no doubt about it. This card means feeling affected by all the negative thoughts in your head. This kind of energy divides and drives away what was once united. You lose your bearings, and everything becomes a bit inflexible.

Reversed meaning: Curiosity, verbosity, an intuitive intellect, a passion for words. Watch out: what you say can come back to bite you!

Reading: You feel everything is personal. You find it difficult to relate to others. That's why you keep your distance. You believe you were deceived, that there's betrayal all around. This is painful, but it will make you stronger.

THREE OF SWORDS

THREE OF CUPS

Abundance: Three women raise their cups in celebration. What will you drink to? Fulfilment. When the group gets together, they find a name for it, they send each other funny memes and remember old times. These meetings are rituals of abundance.

Reversed meaning: Success can be brief. In its negative aspect, this card means inner debate between the things that are not important and the big topics that motivate you.

Reading: It's time to share. Sharing leads to better things. The people around you are key. Prioritize your gang.

THREE OF PENTACLES

Teamwork: A woman is hanging a picture in her house. Another one helps her to align it properly. How inspiring is your space? You may not be a fan of meeting up with your neighbours, but in this case you need cooperation. The energy of this card calls for working together to make things better.

Reversed meaning: Economic weakness. Biting off more than you can chew. Hyperactivity or a useless partnership.

Reading: Start the game. Share experiences, ask for help, exchange tips. All this will help you reach your goal.

Three is a dynamic number that expresses outward. It represents starting to grow.

FOUR OF WANDS

Putting things into practice: The card shows a couple welcoming others under a gate that appears to lead to their house. Four wands and a floral banner are visible at the entrance. This card means you can finally have something you have always dreamt of. Receive this new possibility with enthusiasm.

Reversed meaning: A repeated pattern. There is monotony in the security of the number four, but it is about knowing how to act in this situation so that it does not have an unusual effect on you.

Reading: Everything settles down. It may be your family, your work or your emotions. The state of mind is serene, as in Temperance.

FOUR OF WANDS

FOUR OF SWORDS

Truce: Four swords float above a resting girl. We cannot tell if she is meditating, praying or taking a nap. But, in the meantime, you can wonder about what resting means to you. This card represents intellectual maturity: knowing when to step aside and leave the conversation. Arguing until everything blows up brings with it a dose of adrenaline. This card proposes the opposite.

Reversed meaning: Being too conservative, only dealing with what is necessary, lacking passion. These are some of the traps of this card.

Reading: Take it easy. Take some time out and then you will be able to reorganize your material life. This card represents a practical mind. You need to recuperate before going back to action.

FOUR OF SWORDS

FOUR OF CUPS

Apathy: A girl sitting by a tree sees three cups but chooses none of them. She is holding the fourth cup but doesn't look very satisfied. Is she picky or is it a whim? It is neither one nor the other. This card means you are not convinced by anything you are offered. Such lack of interest is close to lack of any feeling. If we're not careful, it can lead to being closed off from others.

Reversed meaning: Being comfortable at home with your routine. What happens when you leave those four walls?

Reading: If you feel you get nothing in return or nothing appeals you, you may be going through an identity crisis. What happens if somebody tells you that most of these worries are temporary?

FOUR OF CUPS

FOUR OF PENTACLES

Possession: Three golden coins surround a woman who is holding on tightly to a fourth one. This card is an invitation to think about your relationship with your possessions. Do you think life is a zero-sum game, in which one person's gain is another's loss? If you don't turn this around, it will lead to the inevitable break represented by Five of Pentacles. Try to think of win-win situations, in which no one has to lose in order for others to win.

Reversed meaning: Greed, stubbornness and not seeing other people's needs. An inability to accept what you receive from others.

Reading: You need to give in order to receive. If you have the resources, circulate them: donate your clothes, share your work, buy local. You can build virtuous circles that mean more people will win.

FOUR OF PENTACLES

The number four speaks of a stability that we should leave behind, be it sooner or later. This number means structure.

FIVE OF WANDS

Trial and error: A group are fighting with their wands, but the scene does not suggest violence. Are they trying out different points of view? The fight is provoked by different interests. Number five always represents the act of seeking knowledge in order to progress.

Reversed meaning: We exaggerate to blur the boundary between our inner world and outer selves. In its negative aspect, this card may suggest somebody is talking without thinking about their words. The inner fire we saw in the Ace of Wands is now manifesting and it can leave the whole group in flames.

Reading: You know you are creating a conflict that could be avoided. Ask yourself whether that path leads to more losses than victories.

FIVE OF WANDS

FIVE OF SWORDS

Struggle: We can see the sea in the background and two women retreating, exhausted. The woman in the front holds the swords and worries about the scene she sees. Is this winning? Win or lose, this battle feels like a defeat. It's not that something was lost, but, at the end of the day, we know we have hurt ourselves more than we have hurt anybody else.

Reversed meaning: Within a group, somebody has very clear ideas that differ from the rest. In its negative aspect, this card may mean that person is trying to convert everyone to their opinion. New people may be useful.

FIVE OF SWORDS

Reading: Arrogance may take hold of you and do you harm. If you can't get anyone to see how brilliant your idea is, it may be time to rethink. Be encouraged to give way.

FIVE OF CUPS

Insight: The card shows a woman turning her back on us. We see her head down, lost among the broken and overturned cups around her. Wounds from the past are coming to the surface. Something triggers a sorrow that seems inexplicable right now. Cups are nostalgic and speak of your teenage years; they ask you to make room for them deep inside.

Reversed meaning: When feeling vulnerable, it's only natural to trust in something and delve into it. Extreme views may lead you to blindness, making it even more difficult to emerge from this state.

Reading: You have the chance to express your pain, as old as it may be. Look for support. Choose a modest life. Renew your faith in yourself.

FIVE OF CUPS

FIVE OF PENTACLES

Against all odds: A girl and her dog walk along, casting a shadow on everything around them. The scene suggests misery and deprivation. The withered flowers in the card suggest negligence. But the people are moving. Will they move on against all odds? We all have problems, but they become more serious when we've spent too much time trying to numb them. This card means that you are hitting rock bottom in an area of your life, be it work, health, relationships or your personal life.

Reversed meaning: A new strategy to overcome a crisis. In reverse, this card means you can solve a problem, but it will require a lot of effort.

Reading: If you are unhappy with your current situation, do something to change it; start composting, learn about renewable energies, have a Tarot reading or simply learn something new.

FIVE OF PENTACLES

Unstable by nature, number five suggests a transition that's difficult to avoid.

SIX OF WANDS

Victory: A woman wearing a crown of flowers rides a bike and contemplates the landscape around her. This card suggests your actions may be rewarded. The movement in the image is a moment of freedom, coming together and reconciliation. Although some things may be delayed, everything will happen in due time. Falling in love with your surroundings is a virtue, as in The Lovers.

Reversed meaning: The road is slow; you need to be receptive to your environment and you probably won't stand out too much.

Reading: Do you know all the possibilities ahead? Do you remember The Lovers' challenge to choose without losing? In this case, you have chosen wisely. Enjoy this small, personal victory.

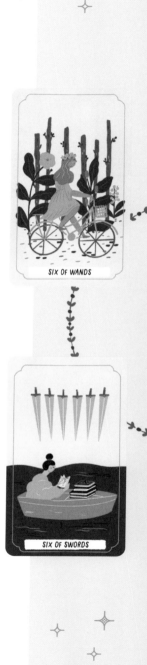

SIX OF WANDS

SIX OF SWORDS

Retreat: In this card, we have a water scene: a woman is sailing away on a raft. In the Four of Swords, intellectual maturity asked for a break. Now it asks for distance. In order to rebalance your strength, this card asks you to move, either physically or emotionally.

Reversed meaning: Intellectual narcissism. Being in love with your own ideas may lead to loneliness.

Reading: In Five of Swords, you fought and got hurt. Calling a truce is not losing if it helps you feel better. Even if you have not convinced everybody of your idea, it's time to retreat and think on your own.

SIX OF SWORDS

SIX OF CUPS

Nostalgia: Two girls exchange flowers in a spring-like environment. There's a popular saying: "Growing old is mandatory; growing up is optional." This card reunites you with your inner child. The answer lies with those teachers, classmates and childhood memories.

Reversed meaning: Re-living and not letting go of past mistakes. In reverse, this card means looking forward to things you promised yourself when you still had a naive view of the world.

Reading: Poetry, art, everyday beauty. Treat yourself with tenderness and respect the joy of the nostalgia this card may invite you to experience.

SIX OF CUPS

SIX OF PENTACLES

SIX OF PENTACLES

Balance: Two friends have tea in the afternoon. They seem to be enjoying an exchange of simple gifts, chosen with love. There's joy because there's balance. After the misery of Five of Pentacles, you are reborn and acknowledge everyday miracles. Everything is enjoyed, from a tasty breakfast to a warm bed.

Reversed meaning: The system of values is confused. It's not clear who gives and who takes. This confusion may lead to obsession.

Reading: Rotation. If you usually give, it's time to receive. If you always receive, it's your time to share. This new circulation flows. There's prosperity, especially in the world of art and culture.

Six is a hedonistic number that suggests seduction is a natural consequence of being connected to ourselves.

SEVEN OF WANDS

Courage: A barrier made of seven wands tries to stop the main character on this card. Are you willing to lead the way? This card is an invitation to confront it all. Your desires may become a battlefield. Take care: you may end up swimming against the current and expending more energy than necessary.

Reversed meaning: When in doubt, be on guard. Being on the defensive all the time does not serve your purpose.

Reading: Face the music. Don't quit before it's your time. You should reinforce your convictions as you move forward. No pain, no gain.

SEVEN OF SWORDS

Audacity: A woman seems to be leaving, carrying several swords. Do they belong to her or has she stolen them? This card suggests that when you bite off more than you can chew you become overwhelmed and lose balance. Such pressure may lead to lies and other ways of hiding the truth so as not to show how overwhelmed you are. Wake up. You've been found out.

Reversed meaning: When there are no bad intentions, this card speaks of the pinnacles of success and invites you to share your wisdom with your community.

Reading: There's a hidden strategy. Swords are sharp and someone may end up hurting themselves. When this card appears in a reading, some people say that ideas have been stolen. Others say that thoughts that have been passed down are heavy. The advice is to meditate on this warning.

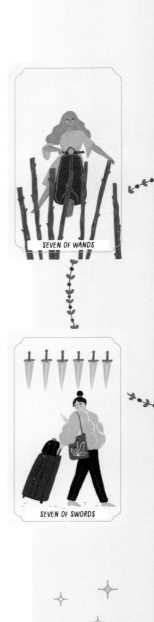

SEVEN OF WANDS

SEVEN OF SWORDS

SEVEN OF CUPS

Illusion: Seven cups float in a dreamy cloud, offering multiple temptations: relics, balance, trips, lust, time. What is your fantasy? The perfect soundtrack for this card would be "Lucy in the Sky with Diamonds". We don't know exactly what this song is about, but it makes us float. This card has a dreamy energy.

Reversed meaning: If universal love and kindness are there for me, let them be there for everyone.

Reading: Fiction alert. The sensation may be wonderful, but it's all in your head. You are attracted to mirages and fall into the temptation of a mysterious utopia that won't make any sense in a month or two.

SEVEN OF CUPS

SEVEN OF PENTACLES

Anxiety: A girl is watching her cacti and succulents grow. She can't see any progress and is disappointed. This card suggests hunger for results. Not willing to give things the time they need, you jump to conclusions and think that things have failed. This card is related to the seventh arcanum, The Chariot. Don't ride it frenetically.

Reversed meaning: Disregarding spiritual life, being prejudiced without even trying things out.

Reading: The wait is worthwhile. The fruits of your labour are on their way. In order to understand the strength of spiritualized matter, you need to accept the natural cycle of things, even if it sounds boring.

SEVEN OF PENTACLES

Although seven has a reputation for getting projects done, there's always a secret agenda.

EIGHT OF WANDS

Multitasking: Eight wands fly toward the ground like rays of light. Where do they find you? Do you think you will be able to hold them off or are you ready to dodge them? Many things are happening at the same time and there are all kinds of trouble. Issues are approaching fast. In some cases, they briefly overwhelm your environment. How should you behave in the face of so many stimuli?

Reversed meaning: Energy comes together and something is created. All the wands move in your favour.

Reading: When this card appears in a reading, we should multiply the energy of The Magician by eight. That's a lot, isn't it? But keep in mind: sometimes multitasking and doing so much means not achieving anything.

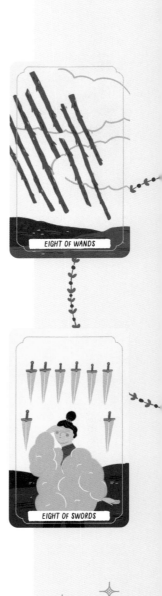

EIGHT OF WANDS

EIGHT OF SWORDS

EIGHT OF SWORDS

Self-criticism: A blindfolded girl seems tied to her own vision of the world (or lack of it). It's time for reflection. Somebody has become stuck in their ideas and is not able to receive any new messages. This attitude means being in denial. You are criticized and are locked in a vicious circle. This energy is experienced like the dark side of Justice.

Reversed meaning: The reverse meaning of this card is perfect for meditation. In a deep trance, we manage not to think – what a relief!

Reading: This card speaks of an intellectual block and calls for a return to the basics. First, escape the noise of interference and then take advantage of the blindfold to look inside yourself and solve the puzzle.

EIGHT OF CUPS

Putting two and two together: With the same energy of The Hermit, but in an earlier stage, a girl retreats in the peace of this scene of eight cups. Not even the victories of number seven are worth thinking about. A daydream has come to an end and reality hits you in the face. You change your perception. What have you lost? What have you won? Boundaries blur before you can move forward.

Reversed meaning: Leaving without a fight. Abandoning any chance of success without confronting anybody or considering the needs of others.

Reading: Look for new ways of understanding that an emotional process is ending and the past must be left behind. Time, and a good dose of being alone, will bring comfort to your life.

EIGHT OF CUPS

EIGHT OF PENTACLES

EIGHT OF PENTACLES

Goldsmithing: Eight pentacles are meticulously carved, like that friend who does nail art with a steady hand. Practice makes perfect. Mastery means loving the process and respecting the time it takes. Effort and subtlety of detail end up creating a work of art. Which one is yours?

Reversed meaning: You get lost in detail and obsess over errors, becoming an insatiable perfectionist.

Reading: In order to have the life you always dreamt of, you don't have to live the way you were brought up. Honouring life is not the same as living it.

Eight means balance in all aspects. Strength and adjustment. Maturity.

NINE OF WANDS

Warning: The card shows eight firmly planted wands. A girl is holding the ninth wand, while watching something. This card speaks of inner responsibility. For some reason, you cannot lower your guard. All the strength of the wands has been removed. Are you exhausted? You start to feel burdened, as does The Hermit.

Reversed meaning: A lack of productivity, or complaining because you don't have the time, the money or the energy.

Reading: It's true, things are slowing down, but you need to appreciate that you are still on your feet. Turn to your perseverance, a tool you didn't need before but which now gives you the push you need to achieve your goal.

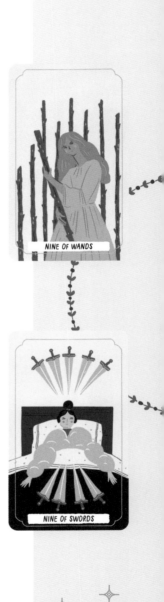

NINE OF WANDS

NINE OF SWORDS

NINE OF SWORDS

Cruelty: The energy of this card is like waking up in the middle of the night after having a bad dream. In the Eight of Swords, you were blindfolded. Here you are immersed in a parallel world you ended up believing in. Nobody thinks those horrible things about you. Wake up from the nightmare you created for yourself.

Reversed meaning: It's good practice to take on other people's ideas. Stubbornness is a very lonely road.

Reading: You are not what you think you are. The mind can play tricks on us sometimes. Maybe it's time to go to therapy or start a physical activity to empty your head a bit.

NINE OF CUPS

Satisfaction: The card shows nine cups arranged around three or four of your belongings: a book, a coffee, your cat sleeping and your favourite song playing. Do you need anything else? A full stomach, a happy heart. You are satisfied with what you have. You have learned to enjoy yourself. This card suggests emotional development. It's time to stop the emotional dependence that is represented by the cups.

Reversed meaning: Excessive consumerism. We said a book, a coffee and your favourite song. Wanting to have a whole library, going from bar to bar or becoming a shopaholic exceeds the notion of healthy fulfilment.

Reading: Do you realize that you can be happy with yourself? That's the goal.

NINE OF CUPS

NINE OF PENTACLES

NINE OF PENTACLES

When life gives you lemons, make lemonade: The card shows nine pentacles and a beaming girl with a little bird, a symbol of freedom, tattooed on her arm. This card suggests full expansion. Growing up was not so boring after all; especially if you consider all the resources at your disposal right now. If you give and take and give again, the passing of time is a victory.

Reversed meaning: Not accepting the passing of time. Always seeing the glass as half empty leads to a bitter old age. In reverse, this card may also suggest you are envious of other people's supposedly perfect lives.

Reading: We are not what time has done to us. We are what we have done with time. Like The Sun, this card confirms the success of taking things forward. The question is: how will you make it last?

Nine represents crisis: learning, growing up, sharing and letting go.

TEN OF WANDS

Oppression: A woman carries ten heavy wands in her rucksack. Could she possibly carry anything more? The most spiritual of the wands comes to the top and looks for a replacement. You need all your wishful strength to be channelled in an idea. The natural order leads us to the beginning of the next suit: the Ace of Swords.

Reversed meaning: As with Wheel of Fortune, in its negative aspect, this card means you will succeed at the project you've put your heart into. Your environment helps you reach the end of the cycle.

Reading: You've assumed all responsibility and now realize you are burdened with things that are not yours. You've come so far, but you can't even celebrate. It would be a good idea to stop dealing with some things.

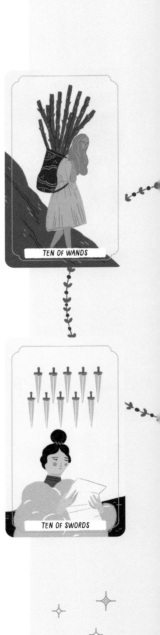

TEN OF WANDS

TEN OF SWORDS

TEN OF SWORDS

Die, ego, die: A woman reads a letter, crying. Is there something you wouldn't like to hear? It turns out that the mind is not all-powerful. Now you need to elevate your thinking and include emotions in your life. That's why this card leads to the Ace of Cups.

Reversed meaning: Fear of getting hurt. You exaggerate your worries and feel broken. Your ideology is in crisis.

Reading: A structural idea falls down, similar to what happens in The Tower. You have to flush out whatever is left. In her book *WTF is Tarot?*, Bakara Wintner says of this card: "Although it's the end of something, it's not your end." Only you are capable of moving forward and being reborn in your emotions.

TEN OF CUPS

Gratitude: An iridescent rainbow of cups shines in the sky. From below, we watch the show, holding hands. This card suggests peace, utter satisfaction and harmony. The celebration is shared because it goes beyond the idea of loving and being loved. This card means total love.

Reversed meaning: Exile, resentment. A family conflict may start when you are afraid of being happy on your own. In reverse, this card suggests you are looking at the celebration from the outside, instead of taking part.

Reading: If nine was joy, ten means being utterly fulfilled. Sisterhood. This card brings about a sense of belonging and prosperity in any relationship.

TEN OF CUPS

TEN OF PENTACLES

System: A girl is receiving her university degree and her parents clap from the first row. What you wished for has happened. You've set something in motion, where everyone played a role and this has worked at full power. This card represents rhythm and group strength. You are in charge and highly empowered.

Reversed meaning: A family system that is too closed makes you rethink some things: your role, your sexual identity, your own forms of personal development. As the Argentine management scholar Alberto Levy would say: "Stand out or die out."

Reading: Full materialization. You are wealthy, but is that all? After this achievement, the material cycle is closed and there's a strong call for creativity. Something has reached its peak. What comes next is the Ace of Wands.

TEN OF PENTACLES

Ten represents the end of a cycle and eternal restart. Culmination.

COURT CARDS

Like the rest of the minor arcana, **pages, queens, kings and knights** are read by combining the role they play with the meaning of their suit. For example, pages have a reputation for being inexperienced, and we know wands have to do with desire. So, a page of wands represents somebody who is starting to experience their desire, maybe in a clumsy way.

   Court cards often represent people from real life. Pages are commonly associated with younger siblings, children or teenagers. Queens are associated with the mother archetype or with an adult woman, while kings often refer to grown-up men, and knights to the figure of a lover or somebody playing a temporary role in our lives. But there's more to it than that. Behind every card there is energy and the figures represent the following:

- **Pages** bring new messages that have not yet proved to be right and they make up a popular social network in which gossip flows. Wherever there are pages there is indecision and a young spirit. Pages are associated with the first, second and third degrees in numerology, especially with the energy of The Magician.

- **Queens** have a strong vision. Enthroned inside their castle, they identify with the element of their suit, looking right at it. Queens cannot help but feel and cling to their nature. In numerology, they are associated with the fourth and fifth degrees – for example, The Emperor.

- **Kings** have power and offer security. They are characterized by their outlook. Kings are the authority that sets boundaries, controls the kingdom and is always ready to act. In numerology, they are associated with the sixth and seventh degrees, behaving in a similar way to The Chariot.

- **Knights** represent freedom. They come and go, sharing what's inside with the outside world. They trade with others and solve problems. Wherever there are knights, everything changes quickly and crises can be triggered. Knights come last because they look toward the energy of the next suit. They are associated with the eighth, ninth and tenth degrees, and cards like Wheel of Fortune.

PAGE OF WANDS

Drive: A handsome young man, a bit rustic in style, stands upright, holding his wand, symbolizing enthusiasm for new adventures. The desire is strong, but it's not clear how to channel it. Creative and sexual energies are at their peak, like a teenager coming to life.

Reversed meaning: Precocious and clumsy, this character may be incapable of resisting his own urges. In reverse, this card warns about a premature stage in which something is spoiled because of an inability to control over-eagerness.

Reading: Amateur seduction. You flirt with an idea or person without much confidence. Wands are felt in the gut. Also, a question is asked: what part of your body makes you proud?

PAGE OF WANDS

PAGE OF SWORDS

PAGE OF SWORDS

Ideas: This is a geekier arcanum. She poses with her sword as a symbol of her intellect. What ideas lurk in the back of your mind that have not yet been given a chance? Ideas are rough diamonds: there would be nothing without them, but at the same time, they won't prosper unless we work on them.

Reversed meaning: Someone who is too talkative or has contradictory thoughts. They may resort to lies or provoke gossip when they feel they are underestimated.

Reading: It is said that an idea is worth 10 per cent, and the remaining 90 per cent is its execution. At this point, the value of your idea is not yet known. The card's advice is not to boast, not to talk too much about it. Don't judge yourself either.

PAGE OF CUPS

Martyr: Beauty, fantasy, idealization. This arcanum carries the idea of a muse, loyalty and devotion. It represents the butterflies in your belly when somebody seduces and touches your heart. The emotional connection is real, but nothing can promise us the platonic bonds that are dreamt of will come true.

Reversed meaning: In reverse, this card means we are experiencing affection in a painful way and taking on the role of the victim. It's like agreeing to solve somebody else's problem and then complaining about being the one who is always helping everybody.

Reading: What do you expect from your cup? Learn to give without asking for anything in return. Romanticizing ideas only to suffer later is the path to dissatisfaction.

PAGE OF CUPS

PAGE OF PENTACLES

On the way to the start: A young man polishes his pentacle, even though it has not yet borne any fruit. Like Aladdin, he's obsessed with his goal. He sets off, determined and committed, at least for a week. We are excited about starting something we don't yet know if we'll be able to continue, but we have mastered the theory.

Reversed meaning: You want to take all the paths and end up choosing none of them.

Reading: You've been considering taking up these studies for a while – a course, a career, a trip, a change in your diet or business. Make a list of how to begin in one column and add a second column on how to make it last. The seed is already there!

PAGE OF PENTACLES

Pages hold more enthusiasm than knowledge. They search for a sense of belonging.

QUEEN OF WANDS

Fiery: A vital, fiery woman experiences the intensity of life. This queen is in charge of her desires. She knows what she wants and would rather apologize later than ask for permission. She's passionate, sensual and playful. Most of all, she's daring.

Reversed meaning: Sexual or any other kind of obsession. In reverse, this card warns about how Aries energy can lead us to be pushy with others.

Reading: It's time to make decisions based on instinct – and that suits you. Release everything, come into contact with art and fire. Creativity is closer than you think. In this state, you radiate desire.

QUEEN OF WANDS

QUEEN OF SWORDS

QUEEN OF SWORDS

Strategy: This card refers to the archetype of the mother, boss or the perfect student. This queen is usually frowning and making sure everything is in order. A sharp mind organizes the timing and responsibilities of others so that each piece of the puzzle falls into place. The presence of this card speaks of efficiency.

Reversed meaning: The counterpart of this queen is coldness and a reduced outlook. When reversed, this card means you are unwilling to show your wounds and live blindly by your own values. Maybe you are being dogmatic, as in the reverse side of Justice.

Reading: When you judge others, you are internally judging yourself. Pay attention to the final destination of your sharp swords or those of the person who is showing you the way.

QUEEN OF CUPS

Maternal: Powerful and kind, this queen is protective and empathetic without losing her sensuality. She feels comfortable on a sofa, exchanging hugs and warm words. Her dream is to help others. She's loving and caring, and helps those around her.

Reversed meaning: Being extra sensitive and often feeling that the world is against you. In reverse, this card suggests jealousy, psychological games and social rejection.

Reading: You may need advice on love, a hug or a tender gesture. It is allowed. Open up to whoever is willing to listen to your feelings.

QUEEN OF CUPS

QUEEN OF PENTACLES

QUEEN OF PENTACLES

Owner: Gorgeous and successful, her marital status may be "building an empire". This queen is active, visionary, capable of realizing projects and brave enough to innovate in various situations. She's her own boss.

Reversed meaning: Greed or selfishness. A queen who loves herself more than she loves her kingdom cannot reap good results. In reverse, this card may mean that obsession with results can make you lose track of the whole picture. Also, you may be having a hard time accepting the passing of time.

Reading: Defend your treasure, don't lose focus, unfold your wings. The energy of this queen speaks of progress and resources. If you take care of your business, you will find prosperity.

Sensitive, sensual, intense and determined, queens know what they are talking about.

KING OF WANDS

Maturity: This king represents mature, experienced energy, full of enthusiasm and ready to rock. Unlike the Page of Wands, this card suggests control and mastery of passions. This king is the archetype of an honest, creative lover and a talented person. Come what may, he is ready.

Reversed meaning: A tyrannical, seductive lover. In reverse, this card represents someone who makes many promises but keeps none. A self-centred artist, someone who does not see the needs of those around them.

Reading: The challenge is to continue what you have started, something that you are good at. Discipline is hard, but you have the will to achieve it. Find creative ways of seeing your projects through.

KING OF WANDS

KING OF SWORDS

KING OF SWORDS

Ability: Like a philosopher, this thinker is focused and will not stop until he finds the truth. He has a refined mind that aspires to perfection. This card speaks of clarity. It represents someone who is concise and has mastered the talkativeness of the Page of Swords.

Reversed meaning: A tyrant, a dirty politician or a biased judge. In reverse, this card warns about the destructive side of authority, when it shows no mercy. Avoid verbal aggression.

Reading: Knowledge is your ultimate goal. Everything can be solved by thinking. What are the boundaries that have damaged you? Can they be expanded a bit? Logic is on your side. It's time for assertive decisions.

KING OF CUPS

Patron: A king appears to the world at his most collaborative. Like a Sagittarius grandfather who is kind and optimistic, this person serves others. He knows how to give good advice at the right time. He's understanding and plays a benevolent role when he finds a cause that he can identify with.

Reversed meaning: When you are aware of your influence, you may end up manipulating others. In reverse, this card warns you about someone who is being hypocritical about what he does.

Reading: What views have you inherited from others? What views are your own? The road to wisdom means leaving the cup open, to control how much you give and how much you take. Exchange is enriching.

KING OF CUPS

KING OF PENTACLES

Philanthropist: The archetype represented by this card is a businessman who is wise enough to let go of a part of his wealth in order to start a foundation to improve other people's lives. What is left after you've conquered everything? This king achieved his goals: he's a strategist, merchant and hard worker. Now that he lives in prosperity, he can make his profits flow again.

Reversed meaning: Focusing on your tasks without acknowledging other people's problems. Wanting to earn something without any kind of effort. Becoming stubborn and not accepting outside help.

KING OF PENTACLES

Kings are proactive and capable of managing their domain with different degrees of authority.

Reading: What you touch can turn into gold. You should learn to distinguish between what is important and what is urgent, good problems and real problems. It's time to grow up and be responsible.

KNIGHT OF WANDS

Spirit: This card represents the vigour of a person who is capable of anything in order to take on an adventure. His horse is in a pose; seduction is part of this theatrical performance. Confidence and creativity are channelled into real purpose. This knight is characterized by his ability to master his own desire. He's ready to enter the kingdom of thought: swords.

Reversed meaning: A dilemma that is similar to the one in Strength: how to master your instincts without hurting anybody. Relentless passion can be brutal. And, even though this horse is the most honest of the four, in reverse this card warns about the risk of being ignored if someone puts their own eccentric wishes first.

Reading: There's fun, movement, fire and exploration. The challenge is to make this willpower last.

KNIGHT OF WANDS

KNIGHT OF SWORDS

KNIGHT OF SWORDS

Velociraptor: A jockey rides a horse, as if her life depends on it. Intellectual, effective and brief, this is the archetype of the hardened warrior. She will achieve her goal, no matter what.

Reversed meaning: In reverse, this card warns about a person who always thinks they're right. This is the kind of person with whom heated discussions end badly. They cling to their line of thought, which makes relationships tense, and are not used to giving in.

Reading: This card suggests you can handle things far better than you think. Your strategy has deep roots and, after so much action, this knight tells you that you are ready to connect with your feelings.

KNIGHT OF CUPS

Devotion: Handsome and blushing, this king is not the manliest person around. He may be the most affectionate, though. He could be an activist for peace. The road is more pleasant when we are in sync with our feelings. Kind and idealistic, this card speaks about being useful to others. Charity is your thing.

Reversed meaning: This card warns about a person who loves and regrets, someone who may be self-conscious or jealous, or who gossips about things that are not true.

Reading: Don't force your destiny, let it flow. This horse invites you to take a stroll rather than to try and conquer something. The path of love and healing seems to be its way.

KNIGHT OF CUPS

KNIGHT OF PENTACLES

New horizons: The horse marches steadily and its knight carries a pentacle, as does the ace of the same suit. He's looking for the right time and place to give it away. In his search, he'll find that after succeeding in earthly things he has to look to spiritual matters: he is heading toward wands. With the king, you've already brought projects to fruition. Now, it's time to focus on reconnecting with your desire.

Reversed meaning: When anxiety causes a mental block, and you are juggling many things, problems can arise. The result is a loss of time or resources.

Reading: It's time to look for new things to motivate you. The search does not come to an end or tire you out, but you need to work with others. This card means you have overcome material obstacles and are ready to try new territories.

KNIGHT OF PENTACLES

Moving energy. Knights are proud to accomplish their missions.

READINGS

In order to read the cards, the most important thing is not to know by heart the meaning of all 78 arcana, **but to understand the question you are asking the Tarot, whether it's yours or somebody else's.** The key to asking questions in evolutive (not predictive) Tarot is not to expect a "yes" or "no" answer or to be eager to know how things will end up. In this chapter, we'll talk about ways of approaching the cards in a friendly but assertive way.

- **If the person is talking about a process**, something that started long ago and will continue in the future, you can use the classical three-card reading. For example: "I want to start a new business, but I don't know if I have the right tools." We draw a card to represent the past, to understand our professional energy up until now. Then we draw a card to represent the present, to describe the current dilemma. Finally, a card for the future will tell us where things are heading. (See page 148 to learn more.)

- **If the question includes a negative phrase,** it means one thing is blocking another, so we can use the block reading. For example: "I've been willing to move houses for months, but I cannot achieve it." We draw a card representing the possibility of moving out and another one to represent what is blocking the project. (See page 150 to learn more.)

- **If the question is about a relationship,** in love, work or friendship, we can use relationship readings. For example: "I'm falling for a friend. Is there room to confess my feelings?" We draw a card to represent the relationship, and two more cards: one to represent the person who is asking the question and the other for the other person involved. What does each card tell you? (See page 152 to learn more.)

- **Finally, if the question is about a general topic**, I recommend the Celtic reading. It may look chaotic, as it involves 11 cards, but it provides a good roadmap to reveal the existential dilemmas of the person who is asking the question. For example: "I'm starting to write and I want to know how to make this my full-time job." (See page 154 to learn more.)

Note: It's also good to start with a one-shot reading. This involves drawing just one card to answer any question, to receive advice or to play with the card of the day.

Three-card reading: past, present and future

- **When to use it:** When you are looking to have a general overview of your energy, the situations you are leaving behind, where you are standing in the present and where you are going.

- **What conclusion to draw:** This reading will show you the impact of things from the past and what to focus on in the future.

- **What cards to use:** Use the major arcana in one pile and the minor arcana and court cards in a separate pile. The major arcana will show you the general overview. The minor arcana will add the details.

- **Process:** Shuffle the major arcana, cut the pile in two, spread out the cards and draw three cards from left to right. Then, do the same with the pile of minor arcana cards and place one card below each major arcana card.

This reading can also be done with the major arcana alone. Just by looking at the card numbers, you can identify whether the energy is growing, stuck or flowing. For example, 4, 10 and 18 would mean that the energy has been getting more complex over time, and it's becoming more abstract or referring to your inner world. We know that, because The Moon (eighteenth arcanum) always looks inwards.

Tip: When a reading involves only a few cards and all of them have the same hierarchy (for example, they are all major arcana) we can add up the numbers in each card to tell us about the silent energy underlying the reading.

How to interpret this reading

"I have several jobs and I want to know if it's time to start doing what I like by myself."

The first card in the reading is The Star. It means you need to share your essence with the world. The reversed side of this card means you are drained, giving too much of yourself, and energy is leaking out from all sides. Six of Cups reinforces this view by showing its naive side, **meaning you think you can do everything and therefore burden yourself with too many activities.**

In the position of the present, The Hierophant calls for focus and recognition of the knowledge you already have or acquired not long ago. Maybe it's not time to decide (as Two of Swords seems to advise), but **there is an idea growing within you that needs to keep expanding.**

In the last position, The Magician and Five of Cups speak of your biggest fears: they warn you that, in the future, you will have to face uncertainty, adventure and taking risks. **There is no perfect time.** You need to accept that idea and move forward despite it. Remember that perfect is the enemy of good. You need faith to surrender to this change.

Tip: In this case, the numeric synthesis would be 17 + 5 + 1 = 23. As 23 is after 22 (the number of major arcana), we reduce it again: 2 + 3 = 5. The result is five, which leads us to the energy of The Hierophant, making itself present in this reading again. What underlies this situation is a transitional crisis, which may be solved by taking the risk of starting something from scratch.

Block reading

- **When to use it:** When you want to solve a particular problem and need to see what is blocking you.

- **What conclusion to draw:** This reading shows what may be causing a problem and offers advice on how to solve it.

- **What cards to use:** You can use the whole deck, although the reading is also effective using only the major arcana.

- **Process:** Shuffle the cards, spread them out and draw two cards. The first one is placed horizontally, and it represents your fears or blockages. The second one, placed vertically on top of the first one, represents the way to overcome the stagnant energy.

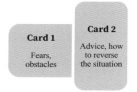

Card 1
Fears, obstacles

Card 2
Advice, how to reverse the situation

Tip: The blocked card is considered in its negative aspect, while the advice is interpreted in a positive way. A typical example of this reading would be a horizontal Fool blocked by The World (vertical). In that case, we would say that The World speaks of a wish to remain in a state of ecstasy, which is locking you up, making The Fool unable to move freely or help you achieve your potential.

This reading can also be used to provide advice on how to dismantle that block. That is to say, how to take card one (blocked) from under card two. If you manage to connect to the more positive version of card two, then card one will become more positive too. So, in this example, if you can celebrate the moment of achievement (The World) without clinging to it, then you will be able to follow The Fool humbly down new paths where adventure awaits.

How to interpret this reading

"In line with the previous reading, I want to know how to manage my energy in order to not be so tired and not to give all my energy away, as The Star suggests in its reversed meaning."

The luminous side of Temperance cannot unfold because the dark side of The Lovers is blocking it. The reading indicates that as you want it all and cannot focus in order to choose one thing to do (The Lovers), you are on your way to emotional unbalance (Temperance). The reading can then be used to provide advice on how to dismantle this block. If you can manage to focus on one task that is fulfilling (The Lovers), then you will find harmony in your routine and you will no longer waste energy, as Temperance suggests.

 Tip: We can always turn to numerology for a clearer interpretation: Temperance is four and The Lovers is six. Remember: four suggests consolidation and stability, while six is about looking for beauty. When number six is blocking number four, you are unable to choose the most beautiful path. As a result, you will feel weak. This explains why you are tired after trying to juggle multiple jobs or projects.

Relationship reading

- **When to use it:** When you want to shed light on a situation between two people. They may be a couple, a pair of friends, a boss and an employee, two relatives, etc.

- **What conclusion to draw:** This reading helps you see what each person is offering or holding back in the relationship.

- **What cards to use:** This reading is effective using the major arcana.

- **Process:** Shuffle the cards, spread out the deck and draw three cards: one for the person who is asking, one representing the general energy of the relationship, and a third showing the energy of the other person involved.

Card 1

The person asking for the spread

Card 2

The relationship's energy

Card 3

The other person in the couple

Tip: Before you start you can split the deck into a pile of major arcana cards and a pile of minor arcana cards. After shuffling and cutting both piles, you can draw two minor arcana to see more details about each person in this reading. These two minor arcana will be placed below cards one and three. It is important to observe the suit of these cards, as this will indicate the energy these people are in contact with and if there is any spark between them.

This reading will not tell you what to do, but it will offer a wider overview to help you understand where you are.

How to interpret this reading

A woman asks me about her relationship with her husband, to whom she has been married for exactly ten years. They have no children and each time they are in crisis they solve it by taking a long trip, which keeps them together for a while longer.

This reading has an interesting analysis. Every time The World appears in a reading, people celebrate. But here, the card is suggesting the opposite: the couple are locked in, with both people looking to stand out individually, and the relationship about to come to an end. Everybody else is also looking at them: their relatives, neighbours and friends are all giving them advice about whether they should stay together or not. These are the figures surrounding The World on the card. It is important to remember that even the most luminous cards have a shadow, a reverse meaning, as is happening in this reading.

The woman is in a state of confusion and feeling very sensitive. This leads her to consult the Tarot, looking for alternative ways in which to channel her emotions. On the other hand, she is stuck and cannot see a solution at the end of the road. She feels she has gone a long way with her husband. Breaking up would make them both lonely and that terrifies her.

On his part, her husband does not seem too involved with his emotional aspect. Strength is a card of leadership, endurance and losing yourself in your own business. He is turning his back on the conflict. It's not that he does not care about it, but his defence mechanism is to deal with other things, maybe more material ones, which makes my client even more confused.

Tip: I advise not to judge people by the cards that represent them, as they only describe their attitude in a particular moment. As Tarot readers, we should not make statements indicating that there is only one option, and we should interpret each person's energy with respect for their context.

Celtic reading

- **When to use it:** When you need a thorough reading of a current situation. Rather than just considering a question, it looks at a whole theme.
- **What conclusion to draw:** This reading allows you to make various associations and consider many ideas. In order to achieve this, you need to pay attention to repeated numbers, predominant suits, the major arcana and, above all, the advice the universe offers.
- **What cards to use:** This reading is most effective using the whole deck.
- **Process:** Shuffle the cards, cut the deck in two, spread out the deck and draw 11 cards to be placed in the following order:

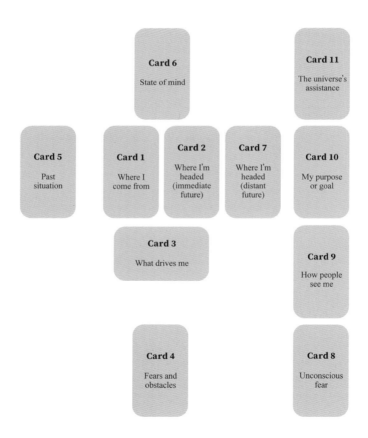

How to interpret this reading

A colleague asked me about a personal problem she was dealing with in therapy: she was concerned about her relationship with her friends. I suggested making a map of her friendship field.

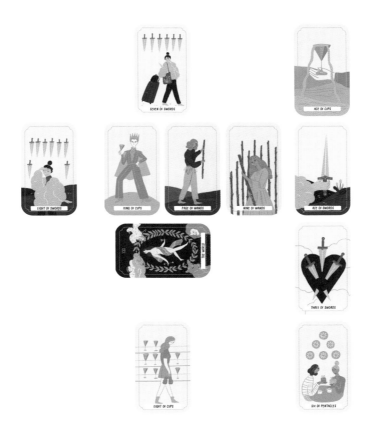

The first question that came to my mind was: "How do you think your parents and your partner feel about this issue?" **The central position represented by the King of Cups and the Page of Wands makes The World a bit dizzy.** The World represents my colleague, locked up by a rigid idea of how friendship works. She had been raised by a super-busy mother who underestimated the value of friendship. As a result, this girl promised herself she would have a lot of friends throughout her life. The Eight of Swords represents the self-imposed order coming from the past; the Seven of Swords speaks about the need to form her own strategy, while the Eight of Wands tells her about the multiple resources at her disposal to solve the issue. But, according to Eight of Cups, down below, she is afraid of being different. **This diamond of sevens and eights indicates that her problem is caught up in a loop.**

According to the Three of Swords, other people see her pain. The Ace of Swords sets a clear goal: she needs to solve the problem from its root. **The pearl of this reading is The Star: her ability to love will help her solve the problem. It doesn't matter who she gives love to, the universe is creating a net to contain her. Her protective energy will soon find others to shelter.**

Note: My colleague was shocked by how deep the reading was and was excited by the idea of further exploring this topic in her life.

Final words

If someone had told me when I was a teenager that part of my adult life would be devoted to studying and teaching Tarot, I would not have believed them. Although I'm a curious person and always searching for knowledge, I must admit I am also deeply rational. I originally studied management. In the publishing house I run with my partner, I'm in charge of commercial strategies, adding up the numbers. The first few times I had a Tarot reading, I was sure there was a logical or probable explanation for a card to be drawn.

But the question of how I got here doesn't matter as much as why I chose to stay. I found in Tarot an endless world of knowledge through which I made my way thanks to teachers, courses and many books. Seeing decks from different cultures and times broadened my mind. I realized that, far from being dogmatic, this discipline is ancient, free and eclectic. I explored its connection to history, astrology, poetry and myths. I found that Tarot lives among us. The visual aspect has always dazzled me. We can take in a huge amount of information about an arcanum just by looking at it for a few minutes. But what I love most about this divination art is being able to share it with other people. Introducing women to the world of Tarot, women from Argentina, Uruguay, Peru, Chile and Colombia, among other countries, has taken the experience to a whole new level.

After all these years of teaching Tarot, I understood that you never know enough. I know that "doubt is one of the names of intelligence" (Jorge Luis Borges) and that the way to wisdom is truly a journey of humility. I believe each of my students has taught me as much as I have taught them. I have also been able to confirm two things. One is that archetypes do exist. People's worries and dilemmas are exactly the same across the world. Another is that nobody needs a wand to do magic: the power of changing reality is within each and every one of us.

Mara Parra

Credits

Josefina Schargorodsky, illustrator | @josefinaschargo

By working on this book, I have achieved a goal I'd had for a very long time: to illustrate a complete Tarot deck. I felt a huge responsibility toward the team, Tarot students and myself. I am terrified and fascinated to know these cards will be in so many hands. I will always be thankful to this amazing team of magicians for giving me the opportunity to take on this adventure, for teaching me the secrets of Tarot, and making the best comments and observations that enabled me to connect with this discipline from more than an aesthetic point of view.

Graciela Caprarulo, foreword writer | @viajedelheroe_gra_caprarulo

Writing the foreword is like being the host, standing at the front door, welcoming guests as they arrive at the party. *The Modern Mystic's Guide to Tarot* is a party to which the reader is invited. I felt we needed a book about Tarot to break up the secrecy around it and bring it into everyday life, so that it could become an instrument for dialogue.

Belén Rigou, designer | @rigoubel

By participating in this beautiful project, as a complete novice, I learnt that Tarot is a powerful tool to encourage dialogue between our past, present and future. I loved this invitation to find new meanings by looking inside ourselves. I wish you all a good journey. *Go home,* psychoanalytic therapy.

Victoria Benaim, curator | @vbenaim

Through this project, Mara has brought to life her vision of a clear, creative and clever Tarot deck. I made this journey as an apprentice, but certain that Jose would be able to elevate it with her illustrations. It has been a perfect pairing!

Mara Parra, author and editor | @marrabelen

First, I wrote this for myself. Then, I wanted to share it. In the end, I put together a team of magicians to make that happen. I studied with Karen Díaz. She taught me that Tarot is more than telling stories: it's melting into images and sailing through their sensitive domain. I reached a point at which my intuition and words came together to describe the world. Would you like to find yours?

ENCHANTRESS TAROT: An Empowering Oracle Deck to Help You Embrace Your Feminine Energy

Text by Mara Parra

Illustrations by Josefina Schargorodsky

ISBN: 978-1-83799-420-5

Are you ready to receive the magic of the cards?

This beautiful Tarot deck, with bespoke illustrations by Josefina Schargorodsky, will help you gain insight into your past, present and future. With these exquisite cards, embrace the sacred power of the Tarot, channel your feminine power and read the unseen forces that guide your path.

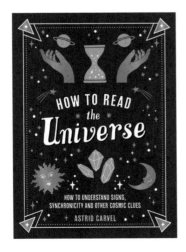

HOW TO READ THE UNIVERSE: The Beginner's Guide to Understanding Signs, Synchronicity and Other Cosmic Clues

Astrid Carvel

Paperback

ISBN: 978-1-83799-191-4

Discover the ancient language of the universe, decipher its messages and unravel its mysteries – all you need is this book and your own intuitive powers. Filled with advice and inspiration, this book will be your essential guide to reading the cosmos, helping you to discover your true path and find both magic and meaning in the everyday.

Have you enjoyed this book?

If so, find us on Facebook at **Summersdale Publishers**,
on Twitter/X at **@Summersdale** and on Instagram
and TikTok at **@summersdalebooks** and get in touch.
We'd love to hear from you!

www.summersdale.com